The Intuitive Entrepreneur

Follow Your Inner Compass to Unlock the Business of Your Dreams

Kristi Smith

Greenlamp Publishing

Published in the United States of America by Greenlamp Publishing, an imprint of Greenlamp LLC, Orange County, California

GreenlampPublishing

30021Tomas, Suite 300

RanchoSanta Margarita, CA 92688

ISBN: 978-1-963977-20-2

Dedication

To the dreamers, the doers, and the seekers of their true path—
May this book serve as a guide and a gentle nudge toward the life you've always imagined.

To my family, whose love, support, and unwavering belief in me have been my greatest strength.

And to every entrepreneur following their inner compass, may you find clarity, courage, and success in every step of your journey.

This is for you.

Contents

CHAPTER ONE

Introduction

YOUR JOURNEY BEGINS

Welcome to The Intuitive Entrepreneur: Building a Purpose-Driven Business That Aligns With Your Soul

This isn't just another business book. This is your call to action—a manifesto for the dreamers, the misfits, the changemakers, and the rebels who know that entrepreneurship isn't just about profits. It's about purpose. It's about creating something meaningful, leaving a legacy, and unapologetically being yourself while building a venture that aligns with your soul.

If you've ever felt like you don't fit the traditional entrepreneur mold, you're in the right place. The world doesn't need more carbon copies. What it needs is YOU—your voice, your vision, and your unique way of making an impact.

Your Journey Begins

Entrepreneurship is more than just a step-by-step process; it's a transformational adventure. It's about discovering who you are, what you stand for, and how you can create something extraordinary.

Imagine embarking on a metaphorical journey through awe-inspiring landscapes, each representing a stage in building your business. We'll traverse the rich savannahs of your passions, where your purpose begins to take shape. We'll climb the mountains of clarity, where your vision comes into focus, navigate the deserts of uncertainty where doubt meets resilience, and finally reach the fertile valleys of creation, where your dreams take root and bloom.

This isn't a journey of rigid formulas or stale business strategies. This is about unlocking your creativity, tapping into your intuition, and crafting a venture that resonates deeply with who you are. By the end of this adventure, you won't just have a business idea—you'll have a clear, purpose-driven plan uniquely yours. A business born from your values, built with intention, and designed to create impact.

The Entrepreneurial Mindset: Becoming the Architect of Your Own Reality

Successful entrepreneurs don't just build businesses—they build worlds. They shape reality through vision, resilience, and unwavering belief in their purpose. But to do that, you must first rewire how you think about success, failure, and possibility.

- **Embrace Discomfort**: Growth happens outside your comfort zone. Every challenge is an opportunity to sharpen your instincts and refine your purpose.

- **Cultivate Resilience**: The entrepreneurial path isn't linear. There will be setbacks, but every obstacle is a lesson in disguise.

- **Adopt a Beginner's Mindset**: The most successful entrepreneurs remain curious, open-minded, and willing to adapt.

- **Lead with Purpose**: Money follows impact. When you build something that serves others, success naturally flows.

Your mindset is your greatest asset. The way you think, perceive challenges, and take action determines the trajectory of your journey. Throughout this book, we'll strengthen that mindset so you can navigate the highs and lows with confidence.

Why This Book? Why Now?

The world is ready for a new kind of entrepreneur: one who leads with heart, creates with intention, and isn't afraid to challenge the status quo. Today, technology has leveled the playing field, making it easier than ever to start a business. But what sets you apart isn't just access to tools; it's your passion, your story, and your intuition.

You don't have to be seasoned or follow a cookie-cutter formula. All you need is a willingness to explore, grow, and trust the compass inside you. If you've ever felt the pull to create something bigger than yourself, something that matters, then this is your moment.

Here's how we'll do it:

- We'll break down the overwhelm of starting a business into clear, actionable steps.

- We'll use your intuition as a compass, guiding you to decisions that feel authentic.

- We'll craft a business that reflects your unique story, not a one-size-fits-all formula.

Lessons from History: Visionaries Who Followed Their Compass

Throughout history, the most impactful entrepreneurs have been guided by more than just profits—they've been driven by passion, curiosity, and a sense of purpose.

- **Steve Jobs**: Before co-founding Apple, Jobs embarked on a transformative journey to India, searching for spiritual clarity and self-awareness. This experience was less about discovering the next technological breakthrough and more about connecting with his true self. His deep exploration of philosophy, meditation, and spirituality influenced his approach to innovation, where intuition and passion guided his vision. Jobs didn't just create products—he created a legacy, intertwining technology with a sense of purpose and beauty.

- **Richard Branson**: With his fearless sense of adventure and unyielding curiosity, Branson turned Virgin Group into a global empire. From launching an airline to dreaming of space tourism, Branson's willingness to take risks and venture into uncharted territory defined his success. His entrepreneurial spirit is rooted in a belief that the best business is one that challenges the status quo, embraces fun, and puts people at the heart of everything. His life's work has been about making bold moves and empowering others to do the same.

- **Madam C.J. Walker**: The daughter of formerly enslaved parents, Walker rose from humble beginnings to build an empire that revolutionized the beauty industry. Her genius wasn't just in creating products; it was in understanding and empowering a community that was often overlooked. She built a brand for women of color, with a focus on self-care, self-love, and independence. Walker's entrepreneurial journey was marked by resilience, defying societal limitations, and showing that the most impactful businesses come from the heart and the desire to uplift others.

- **Nikola Tesla**: Tesla's pursuit of boundless energy and the belief that humanity could tap into free, limitless power was nothing short of visionary. He spent his life inventing and experimenting, often at great personal cost, driven by an unwavering commitment to what he believed was the future of humanity. Tesla didn't create to make money—he created because he believed that technology could unlock humanity's true potential. His work laid the groundwork for the modern electrical world, and his legacy endures as a symbol of innovation fueled by purpose.

- **Malala Yousafzai**: Though her path may not fit the traditional mold of entrepreneurship, Malala is one of the world's most powerful changemakers. After surviving a violent attack for advocating for girls' education in Pakistan, she turned her personal struggle into a global movement. Malala's commitment to education, equality, and the empowerment of girls is her entrepreneurship—transforming passion into a worldwide initiative that continues to inspire generations. Through her work, she's demonstrated that true leadership is born from a deep commitment to a cause larger than oneself.

- **Oprah Winfrey**: From humble beginnings, Oprah built a media empire that goes far beyond just entertainment. Her business acumen is deeply rooted in her personal story of overcoming adversity. Oprah's authenticity, vulnerability, and ability to connect with people on a deeply emotional level transformed her into a global brand. Her life's work isn't just about business—it's about empowering others to discover their own strength and potential. Oprah's entrepreneurial journey is one of using her voice to inspire transformation and create a platform for others to rise.

- **Howard Schultz**: Schultz didn't just build Starbucks; he built a movement that redefined the coffee experience. Growing up in a working-class neighborhood, Schultz was driven by a vision to create a company that would provide not just coffee, but a sense of community and connection. Starbucks became a third place between home and work, a space where people could feel at home, regardless of where they were from. Schultz's approach to business focused on the human element, with values that placed people first, and sustainability as a core principle.

- **Tory Burch**: Starting with a single store, Tory Burch built a global fashion brand by combining style with purpose. Her company became not just a place to shop but a platform for women's empowerment. She created opportunities for women through the Tory Burch Foundation, which provides funding, mentorship, and resources to female entrepreneurs. Tory's business success was not just about fashion—it was about creating a lasting legacy of support, opportunity, and confidence for women in business.

- **Yvon Chouinard**: The founder of Patagonia, Yvon Chouinard redefined what it means to be an entrepreneur in the modern age. Patagonia isn't just an outdoor clothing company—it's a force for environmental activism.

Chouinard's commitment to sustainability and ethical business practices has set the brand apart, showing that success doesn't need to come at the expense of the planet. His approach is proof that businesses can thrive while still doing good for the world and that purpose-driven entrepreneurship is the future.

- **Andrew Carnegie**: Known for his rise from humble beginnings to becoming one of the wealthiest men in the world, Carnegie's entrepreneurial journey was rooted in both ambition and a deep sense of philanthropy. A Scottish immigrant, he worked tirelessly to build his steel empire, yet, in the later stages of his life, he believed that wealth should be used for the betterment of society. Carnegie's legacy is a blend of business brilliance and an unwavering belief in the power of giving back, as he donated the vast majority of his fortune to causes like education, libraries, and peace initiatives. His philosophy that "the man who dies rich dies disgraced" transformed the way the world viewed wealth and responsibility.

- **Cornelius Vanderbilt**: Vanderbilt, known as the "Commodore," revolutionized the American transportation industry, first through railroads and later through shipping. Starting with a small ferry business, he built one of the largest railroad empires in the United States, fundamentally changing how goods and people moved across the country. His approach to business was aggressive, fiercely competitive, and marked by a strong belief in innovation and progress. Despite his wealth and power, Vanderbilt's legacy remains complex, marked both by his ruthless tactics in business and his eventual philanthropy, especially his donation to educational institutions, most notably the founding of Vanderbilt University. His story embodies the power of vision and determination in shaping industries and communities.

What these visionaries shared wasn't just ambition—it was a commitment to their purpose and the courage to act on it. Now it's your turn to follow your inner compass and make your mark.

Your Business Is Unique—Just Like You

Forget the one-size-fits-all advice. Your business isn't a template. It's a reflection of your passions, your values, and the impact you want to create.

Think of two entrepreneurs starting cafés. One envisions a vibrant, community-focused space that hosts local art and live music. The other dreams of a minimalist, high-tech café that delivers a seamless experience for busy professionals. Both visions are valid, but each requires a completely different strategy.

This book honors your individuality. Together, we'll uncover what drives you, and we'll design a business that aligns with your soul.

What You'll Gain

By the end of this book, you'll have more than just a business plan. You'll have:

- Clarity about your purpose and vision.

- A roadmap tailored to your unique journey.

- Confidence to overcome challenges and trust your instincts.

- Strategies to create a business that's meaningful and sustainable.

- A deeper connection to your intuition, allowing you to make decisions that align with your true self.

- A framework for continuous growth, ensuring that your business evolves with you.

More importantly, you'll have the mindset and skills to continue growing long after your initial launch.

Your Notes & Next Steps

At the end of each chapter, you'll find a Notes & Reflection section. This space is for you to jot down insights, ideas, and next steps. Use it to track your progress, capture aha moments, and outline actions that feel aligned with your journey.

Additionally, to help you turn your vision into a structured plan, I've created a **Business Plan Template** that you can access here: **bit.ly/4hbWez1**. This document will walk you through key components of your business strategy, from defining your mission to mapping out financial projections.

Let's Begin

The world needs your vision. It needs businesses built with heart, creativity, and purpose. If you've ever felt the pull to create something that matters, to challenge the status quo, and to leave a legacy, this is your moment.

So, take a deep breath. Trust that you're exactly where you need to be. Pack your metaphorical bags, unleash your creativity, and get ready to step into the adventure of a lifetime. Together, we'll build the business of your dreams—one that's unapologetically, uniquely yours.

The journey starts now. Let's create something extraordinary.

CHAPTER TWO

Preparing for Your Journey...

BUILDING THE FOUNDATION OF YOUR DREAM BUSINESS

"Failing to plan is planning to fail." – Benjamin Franklin

A Journey Begins: Turning Dreams Into Purpose-Driven Reality

Picture this: You're standing at the edge of a vast and breathtaking mountain range, the horizon full of endless possibilities. The air carries a mix of excitement and trepidation, and deep down, you know that the step you take next could shape the rest of your life. This is where every purpose-driven entrepreneur begins—at the crossroads of a big dream and an even bigger unknown.

Think of Sarah's story. She was a corporate professional with a comfortable paycheck, but her work didn't align with her values or her vision for the future. Her heart craved meaning and impact. So, she took a leap into the unknown, leaving behind security for purpose. Her path wasn't without its challenges—she faced financial struggles, sleepless nights, and moments of doubt. But with clarity, passion, and a solid foundation, Sarah transformed her dream into a thriving business that not only fulfilled her but also empowered others.

Like Sarah, you stand on the cusp of your own adventure. This chapter is your guide to laying a foundation strong enough to carry your dream from an idea into a legacy. Let's build something extraordinary.

Step 1: Define Your 'Why' – The Compass of Your Business

Your "why" is more than a motivational mantra. It's the beating heart of your venture, the magnetic force that keeps you moving when the road gets tough. It's the reason your audience will connect with you on a deeper level.

Ask Yourself:

- What change do I want to create in the world?

- Why does this dream matter to me?

- How will my business impact others and leave a lasting legacy?

Historical Inspiration: Consider Rosa Parks. Her courageous act of defiance wasn't just about refusing to give up a seat—it was about igniting a movement. Her "why" wasn't rooted in personal gain but in her unwavering commitment to justice and equality. Similarly, Mahatma Gandhi's dedication to nonviolent resistance led to India's independence, proving that a steadfast purpose can change the course of history.

Your "why" doesn't need to be world-altering on day one, but it should be the light that guides your way. Take the time to reflect on what drives you at your core. This clarity will ground you and differentiate your business in a noisy world.

Step 2: Packing Your Essentials – Passions, Skills, and Strategies

Every great journey requires preparation. The "essentials" for your entrepreneurial adventure include your passions, skills, and the strategies that will sustain you.

Passion:

Passion is your fuel. It's what gets you through late nights, early mornings, and unforeseen detours. Think about what excites you so much that you lose track of time. Passion is non-negotiable—it's the soul of a purpose-driven business.

Skills:

Your skills are your toolkit. These might include tangible abilities like design, writing, or financial management, as well as intangible strengths like empathy, leadership, or resilience. Make a list of your top skills and identify areas where you may need support or growth. Remember, even Steve Jobs needed Steve Wozniak.

Strategies:

Without a strategy, passion and skills are directionless. Begin outlining the steps to bring your vision to life. These can include setting short-term goals, identifying key resources, and planning for sustainability. A flexible but actionable plan is your map for the journey ahead.

Step 3: Market Research – Understanding the Landscape

Market research is like scouting the terrain before setting out. You wouldn't explore uncharted territory without some preparation, and the same goes for launching a business.

Research Your Industry:

- What trends are shaping your field?

- Where are there gaps in the market that align with your strengths and vision?

Understand Your Audience:

Your audience is your guiding star. Who are they? What do they need? How can you help them?

Analyze Your Competitors:

Studying others in your space isn't about comparison—it's about learning. What can you do differently or better?

Historical Perspective: Henry Ford didn't invent the car, but he revolutionized the auto industry by identifying what others were missing: affordability and accessibility. Similarly, Airbnb disrupted the hospitality market by seeing what traditional hotels couldn't—consumers wanted connection and a sense of home.

Another example is Madam C.J. Walker, who became the first female self-made millionaire in America by recognizing an untapped market: hair care products designed for Black women. By addressing a unique need, she built an empire that empowered her community.

Step 4: Learn From the Trailblazers

Throughout history, the most impactful entrepreneurs have dared to chart their own paths.

- **Oprah Winfrey:** From a humble upbringing to building a media empire, Oprah's commitment to authenticity and purpose has been her compass. She reminds us that staying true to ourselves is the ultimate strategy.

- **Sara Blakely:** When Sara invented Spanx, she didn't have a business degree or connections. She had a clear vision, boundless determination, and the courage to solve a problem no one else had addressed.

- **Harriet Tubman:** Known as "Moses" for her role in the Underground Railroad, Tubman's entrepreneurial spirit was rooted in her unwavering commitment to freedom and justice. She risked everything to create a legacy of liberation.

- **Walt Disney:** He was told he lacked imagination early in his career. Yet, his relentless pursuit of a dream led to the creation of one of the most beloved entertainment empires in the world.

What all these visionaries have in common is their ability to trust their instincts, learn from obstacles, and create something that reflects their purpose.

Step 5: Laying Your Foundation

Now it's time to solidify the base of your business.

- **Mission:** Define the purpose of your business in one clear and inspiring statement.

- **Vision:** Envision the legacy you want to create and the impact you'll have.

- **Plan:** Break your dream into actionable steps. Start small, and build momentum as you go.

Ready for the Next Chapter

With your "why" defined, your toolkit prepared, and your research in hand, you're ready to take the first steps into the unknown. In the next chapter, we'll explore how ecosystems like the African savannah can inspire your business model. Just as the savannah thrives on interdependence and balance, so too will your venture require collaboration and adaptability to flourish.

Your adventure is just beginning. The world is waiting for the change only you can bring. Let's take this journey together—and build your legacy, one inspired step at a time.

Action Items – Preparing for Your Journey

To set a strong foundation for your purpose-driven business, take the following actionable steps:

1. Define Your "Why"

- Write down your personal mission statement. Why does this business matter to you?

- Identify the impact you want to create. How will your business make a difference?

- Share your "why" with someone you trust and get feedback on its clarity and emotional power.

2. Take Inventory of Your Strengths

- List your top passions—what excites and motivates you?

- Identify key skills you bring to the table. What do you excel at?

- Highlight areas where you may need to learn or seek support.

3. Conduct Market Research

- Identify 3-5 industry trends that could impact your business idea.

- Create an ideal customer profile: Who are they? What problems do they need solving?

- Research 2-3 competitors. What are they doing well? Where can you stand out?

4. Learn from Trailblazers

- Choose one entrepreneur or leader from this chapter's examples (or another who inspires you).

- Research their journey—what lessons can you apply to your own path?

- Journal about how their story influences your approach to business.

5. Establish Your Business Foundation

- Draft a one-sentence **mission statement** for your business.

- Write a **vision statement** that describes the long-term impact of your venture.

- Identify three immediate action steps to move your idea forward.

6. Access Additional Resources

- Use the **Notes Section** at the end of the chapter to reflect on insights and brainstorm ideas.

- Download the **Business Plan Template** to start structuring your vision into a tangible plan: https://bit.ly/4hbWez1.

Notes & Reflection

17

Notes & Reflection

CHAPTER THREE

Stop #1 – Safari in Africa...

WELCOME TO THE SEAT OF THE WORLD! THE PERFECT PLACE TO START BUILDING YOUR FOUNDATION.

"Go confidently in the direction of your dreams. Live the life you have imagined." – Henry David Thoreau

Stop #1: Safari in Africa – Welcome to the Cradle of Humanity

Where better to begin building your dream business than the birthplace of life itself? The African savannah, with its raw beauty and interconnected ecosystems, offers a living metaphor for the entrepreneurial journey. This is your foundation—your roots—where dreams find purpose and purpose ignites action.

Emma's Awakening: A Journey Toward Purpose

Emma stood in awe on the golden plains of the African savannah, the sun casting a warm glow on the earth teeming with life. This was her reset. A few months earlier, Emma had walked away from her six-figure corporate job, tired of feeling like just another cog in the machine. She wanted something more—a life aligned with her values and work that mattered.

Watching a herd of elephants, Emma saw wisdom in their structure. A matriarch led with grace and strength, while the herd supported one another through the journey. Emma realized that a successful business, like a thriving ecosystem, depends on collaboration, resilience, and intention.

Her mission became clear: to build a purpose-driven venture that honored her skills, passions, and the change she wanted to create in the world. Emma's journey, much like yours, began with defining the why, the how, and the who of her business.

Lesson 1: Tuning Out the Noise – Finding Your True North

In the savannah, every sound has meaning. A rustle of leaves signals a predator, while a bird's call signals safety. Like Emma, entrepreneurs must learn to shut out unnecessary distractions and focus on their inner voice—their true north.

Key Takeaways:

- **Silence the Noise:** The endless chatter of trends and unsolicited advice can drown out your authentic vision. Step away from the chaos to tune into your values.

- **Clarify Your Passion:** Ask yourself what lights you up. What work would you do, even if money wasn't guaranteed?

- **Focus on Impact:** Purpose-driven businesses aren't just about income—they're about the legacy you leave behind.

Example:

Alex, a creative who felt pressure to create trendy products, realized his true purpose was designing sustainable packaging solutions. By silencing external noise, he created a thriving business that supported environmental initiatives and won the loyalty of eco-conscious clients.

Historical Parallel: Consider Galileo Galilei. When the world clung to outdated beliefs, he trusted his observations and revolutionized our understanding of the cosmos. Entrepreneurs, too, must trust their insights—even when others don't yet see their vision.

Lesson 2: Defining Your Mission, Vision, and Values

Sitting under the shade of a mighty baobab tree, Emma started with the fundamentals. If the business is the vehicle, then the mission, vision, and values are the map, compass, and fuel.

Craft Your Mission:

Why does your business exist? Your mission is the heartbeat of your venture—a statement of purpose that drives you forward.

Example: "To empower artisans worldwide by providing a platform to share their crafts, sustain their communities, and celebrate their cultural heritage."

Clarify Your Vision:

What legacy will your business create? Your vision paints the picture of the future you're building.

Example: "To become the leading advocate for ethical trade, transforming global buying habits and uplifting communities."

Define Your Core Values:

These are the principles that guide your every decision. Values shape your brand and build trust.

Example Core Values:

- Sustainability

- Collaboration

- Equity

- Transparency

Historical Inspiration: John Muir, the father of the national parks, had an unwavering mission to preserve nature. His vision and values led to the conservation of vast landscapes, demonstrating the power of a purpose-driven mission.

Lesson 3: Telling Your Story – Your Business Description

Stories have power. They connect, inspire, and influence. Emma knew her business needed a story her audience could believe in.

What to Include in Your Business Description:

- **Business Name:** A name that resonates and aligns with your mission.

- **What You Do:** Clearly outline your product/service and the transformation it offers.

- **Who You Serve:** Define your ideal audience.

- **What Makes You Unique:** Showcase your competitive edge.

Example Description: Savannah Soul Ventures specializes in eco-tourism experiences that immerse travelers in Africa's rich ecosystems and cultures. Our commitment to sustainability, conservation, and local partnerships ensures that every journey makes a lasting positive impact.

Historical Inspiration: Harriet Tubman's legacy was built on storytelling. She didn't just help slaves escape; she inspired hope through her courage, turning her mission into a movement that changed lives.

Lesson 4: Learning from Nature – Lessons in Resilience and Leadership

The savannah's ecosystem thrives on balance, diversity, and adaptability. Each species has a role, and survival depends on collaboration. Business is no different.

Key Wisdom from Nature:

- **Resilience Matters:** The savannah faces droughts, floods, and fires, yet it regenerates stronger than before. Learn to see obstacles as opportunities to grow.

- **Lead with Vision:** Like the elephant matriarch, lead with clarity and confidence while nurturing those around you.

- **Collaborate to Thrive:** No one builds a legacy alone. Surround yourself with mentors, collaborators, and a supportive community.

Historical Inspiration: Nelson Mandela exemplified resilience, emerging from 27 years in prison to unite a nation. His leadership, like that of the elephant matriarch, was rooted in vision and service.

Lesson 5: Choosing the Right Name – A Gateway to Connection

Emma realized the power of a name when she chose "Savannah Soul Ventures." It captured her inspiration while communicating her values of connection, sustainability, and purpose.

Tips for Choosing Your Business Name:

- **Reflect Your Mission:** Make sure your name speaks to your "why."

- **Keep It Memorable:** Simple, unique names are easier to remember and share.

- **Speak to Your Audience:** Your name should evoke emotion and resonate with your target market.

- **Check Availability:** Ensure your name isn't already trademarked or used online.

Example: Nike, named after the Greek goddess of victory, instantly communicates triumph and perseverance.

Lesson 6: Trusting the Process – Embrace the Adventure

As Emma stood on the edge of the savannah one last time, she felt gratitude for the lessons this land had taught her. She knew the road ahead would have challenges, but she also knew she had what it took to succeed.

Remember:

- **Adaptability is Key:** Just as the savannah's animals evolve to survive, your business must remain flexible and innovative.

- **Trust Yourself:** You are the expert of your vision. Trust your instincts.

- **Keep Going:** Every entrepreneur faces setbacks. It's the persistence to rise again that builds legacies.

What's Next? Scaling New Heights in the Andes Mountains

With the foundation laid, it's time to aim higher. In the next chapter, we'll journey to the Andes Mountains, where you'll learn how to map out big-picture goals, develop actionable strategies, and set the stage for long-term growth.

The savannah has prepared you. Your dreams are worth chasing, and the world is waiting for the magic only you can create. Let's go build your legacy.

Action Items — Stop #1: Safari in Africa

To build the foundation of your dream business, take these action steps:

1. Find Your True North — Silence the Noise

- Identify 3 distractions that are pulling you away from your core vision and commit to eliminating or minimizing them.

- Take 10 minutes of quiet reflection (no phone, no social media) to reconnect with what truly excites and drives you.

- Write down your top 3 passions—what would you do even if you weren't paid for it?

2. Define Your Mission, Vision, and Values

- **Mission:** Draft a clear and compelling statement that answers: Why does my business exist?

- **Vision:** Write a future-focused statement describing the legacy you want to create.

- **Values:** Identify 3-5 core values that will guide your decisions and shape your brand.

3. Craft Your Business Story

- Write a one-paragraph description of your business idea. Include:

  - Your business name

  - What you do

- ○ Who you serve

- ○ What makes you unique

- Share your description with a trusted friend or mentor for feedback.

4. Choose a Meaningful Business Name

- Brainstorm 5 potential names that align with your mission and resonate with your audience.

- Research availability (domain names, trademarks, and social media handles).

- Test your top name with a small audience (friends, family, or potential customers).

5. Learn from Nature – Build Resilience & Leadership

- Identify a recent setback and reflect on what you learned from it. How can you use this experience to grow?

- List 3 ways you can build a stronger support system (mentors, collaborators, business communities).

- Commit to one action this week that pushes you out of your comfort zone—growth happens at the edge of challenges.

6. Trust the Process & Keep Moving Forward

- Embrace adaptability—list one way you can remain flexible as your business evolves.

- Trust your instincts—write down a decision you've been hesitating on and take the first step toward action.

- Stay committed—remind yourself of your "why" by reading it aloud each morning.

Notes & Reflection

Notes & Reflection

CHAPTER FOUR

Stop #2 – Soaring to new heights in the Andes Mountains...

GETTING A BIRDS-EYE VIEW TO PLAN OUT YOUR STRATEGY.

"The higher we soar, the smaller we appear to those who cannot fly." – Friedrich Nietzsche

Stop #2: Soaring to New Heights in the Andes Mountains — Gaining a Bird's-Eye View of Your Strategy

Standing at the base of the towering Andes Mountains, Maya couldn't help but feel both awed and intimidated. The jagged peaks seemed insurmountable, yet the condors soaring effortlessly above whispered a deeper truth: perspective is everything.

When Maya started her organic skincare brand, her energy was consumed by the daily grind—perfecting product labels, running social media campaigns, and managing customer feedback. Yet, as months passed, she realized something was missing: a clear, strategic vision. She was buried in the tasks of running her business but hadn't taken a step back to see the bigger picture.

Her journey to the mountains wasn't just a getaway—it was an ascent to a higher mindset. The climb taught her to pause, reflect, and see her business through the lens of possibility, not urgency. Like a condor surveying the vast landscape, Maya realized the importance of stepping back to craft a strategy that would lead her business toward its true potential.

Adopting the Condor's Perspective

In the busyness of entrepreneurship, it's easy to get lost in the weeds. But just as the condor soars above the mountains, the best business leaders rise above the noise to gain clarity.

What does this higher perspective allow you to do?

- **Spot Hidden Opportunities:** What unmet needs or untapped markets are waiting for you?

- **Identify and Close Gaps:** Where are the cracks in your current processes?

- **Anticipate Challenges:** With a wide view, you can prepare for obstacles before they arise.

Imagine the difference between climbing blindly versus climbing with a map. The condor's perspective gives you the clarity to see the entire terrain, making you more intentional and confident in your ascent.

Historical Example: The Incan Road System

The Inca civilization built one of the most advanced road networks in history, spanning nearly 25,000 miles across the Andes. Their ability to plan, adapt, and manage vast distances ensured communication, trade, and military coordination across an empire. Like a visionary entrepreneur, the Incas didn't just focus on individual paths—they saw the entire system and ensured each piece connected to their larger goal.

Designing Your Roadmap: Strategy for the Summit

Once you've gained perspective, it's time to turn that clarity into action. Here's how to map out your strategy:

1. Start with Your Vision: Your North Star

Your vision is the ultimate destination—the summit you're climbing toward.

Questions to Ask Yourself:

- Where do I want my business to be in 5, 10, or 20 years?

- What legacy do I want to create for myself, my team, and the world?

- How will my business impact the lives of others?

Example:

Maya's vision was to create a skincare brand that didn't just care for people's skin but also educated consumers about sustainability. She dreamed of becoming the go-to authority for eco-conscious beauty, setting a new standard for ethical skincare.

2. Break it Down: Goals and Milestones

Big dreams can feel overwhelming, but every summit is reached step by step. Break your vision into manageable milestones.

- **Set SMART Goals** (Specific, Measurable, Achievable, Relevant, Time-bound).

- **Celebrate milestones** along the way to stay motivated.

Example:

Maya's first milestone was to launch a signature Andes-inspired skincare line. Her SMART goal? Achieve $100,000 in revenue within one year while securing three major partnerships with eco-conscious retailers.

3. Audit Your Resources: What's in Your Backpack?

Before you climb, take inventory of your resources:

- **Skills:** What are you great at, and where do you need help?

- **Team:** Who's in your corner, and who else do you need?

- **Capital:** Do you have the funding to sustain your vision?

- **Tools:** Are your systems efficient, or are they holding you back?

Example:

Maya identified her need for better branding and marketing tools. She invested in a graphic designer to elevate her packaging and hired a consultant to streamline her production processes.

4. Execute with Agility

The path to success is rarely a straight line. Be prepared to adapt while keeping your eyes on the summit.

- **Start Before You're Ready:** Perfection is the enemy of progress.

- **Iterate and Improve:** Use feedback from your customers and team to refine your approach.

- **Stay Focused on the Vision:** Let your purpose anchor you when the climb gets tough.

Example:

When Maya faced unexpected delays in sourcing Andes ingredients, she turned the challenge into a marketing moment. She shared the story of working closely with local farmers, connecting deeply with her audience's values.

Historical Example: Ernest Shackleton's Antarctic Expedition

In 1914, Ernest Shackleton led the Endurance expedition to Antarctica. When the ship was trapped in ice, Shackleton adapted, shifting his goal from exploration to survival. His ability to pivot, strategize, and lead under pressure is a testament to the power of resilience and vision. Entrepreneurs, too, must learn when to stay the course and when to pivot to survive and thrive.

The Summit: The Power of Perspective and Strategy

The Andes Mountains teach us that reaching great heights requires more than just determination—it requires vision, adaptability, and strategy. When you take a step back, assess the full landscape, and build a plan, you set yourself up for sustainable success.

Your Action Plan: Building Your Strategy

Here's your roadmap to soaring above the chaos and mapping your way forward:

1. **Create a Strategy Day**: Dedicate uninterrupted time to reflect on your vision and long-term goals.

2. **Write Down Your Summit Goals**: Be bold and specific about what you want to achieve.

3. **Map the Milestones**: Break your big dream into achievable steps.

4. **Audit Your Resources**: Make sure your team, tools, and funding align with your vision.

5. **Commit to Action**: Take the first step today—it's always the hardest but most important.

Next Stop: The Amazon Jungle – Navigating Complexity with Systems and Resilience

After gaining clarity in the heights of the Andes, it's time to step into the wild and unpredictable Amazon Rainforest. This chapter of your journey is all about building the systems, safeguards, and resilience to thrive in an ever-changing world.

From navigating dense foliage to thriving amidst unexpected storms, you'll learn how to create a business structure that not only survives challenges but grows stronger because of them.

Are you ready to take on the jungle? Let's build a foundation that's as resilient as the rainforest itself.

Action Items – Stop #2: Soaring to New Heights in the Andes Mountains

To elevate your business with a clear strategy, take these action steps:

1. Gain the Condor's Perspective – See the Big Picture

- Schedule a **Strategy Day**—block out time to step back from daily tasks and reflect on your business as a whole.

- Identify **three hidden opportunities** in your market that you may not have noticed before.

- List **three current challenges** and brainstorm proactive solutions.

2. Define Your Summit – Clarify Your Vision

- Write down your **long-term vision** (5, 10, or 20 years from now).

- Answer: What impact do I want my business to have? What legacy am I building?

- Ensure your vision is **bold, inspiring, and purpose-driven**—let it be your North Star.

3. Break It Down – Set Goals & Milestones

- Set **one big SMART goal** (Specific, Measurable, Achievable, Relevant, Time-bound).

- Break it into **3-5 milestones** that will move you toward your vision.

- Assign **timelines and accountability** for each milestone.

4. Audit Your Resources – Strengthen Your Climb

- List your **top 3 strengths**—the skills and assets that give you an advantage.

- Identify **gaps**—where do you need support, funding, or better tools?

- Make one decision today to **strengthen a weak area** (e.g., hiring a coach, investing in software, seeking partnerships).

5. Execute with Agility – Take Action

- Take **one imperfect step forward**—start before you feel ready.

- Gather **feedback** from customers, mentors, or your team and adjust accordingly.

- When obstacles arise, ask: **How can I turn this challenge into an opportunity?**

6. Commit to the Climb

- Keep your **vision visible**—write it down and read it daily.

- Set a **monthly check-in** to measure progress and course-correct if needed.

- Stay resilient—remind yourself that every challenge is part of the journey to success.

Notes & Reflection

Notes & Reflection

40

CHAPTER FIVE

Stop #3 – Tour the Amazon Rainforest...

WHERE EVERYTHING IS TRYING TO KILL YOU, PROTECT YOURSELF WITH POLICIES AND PROCEDURES.

"Success is where preparation and opportunity meet." – Bobby Unser

Stop #3: Surviving the Amazon Rainforest – Protect Your Business with Rock-Solid Policies and Procedures

Standing at the edge of the Amazon Rainforest, you're captivated by its lush beauty and endless potential. Yet beneath the towering trees and vibrant wildlife lies a world of challenges: venomous creatures, sudden storms, and unpredictable paths. Survival here demands more than wonder—it requires preparation, vigilance, and an unshakable plan.

Entrepreneurship mirrors this wild terrain. Beneath the excitement of growth and innovation lurk hidden dangers: legal pitfalls, operational chaos, and customer dissatisfaction. Success isn't just about thriving in good times; it's about safeguarding your business against the unexpected.

Take Alex, for example. He started an eco-friendly home goods brand fueled by passion but unprepared for the realities of running a business. A defective product led to a lawsuit, nearly bankrupting him. Only after implementing robust policies—like return protocols, quality controls, and legal safeguards—was he able to rebuild. Today, his business not only survives but thrives, fortified against future challenges.

The lesson from the Amazon? True growth flourishes when beauty is paired with preparation.

Navigating Business Hazards: Lessons from the Jungle

Like the rainforest, the entrepreneurial journey is full of hidden perils that can strike without warning. But with clear policies and procedures, you can mitigate risks and turn obstacles into opportunities. Think of these as your business survival kit:

1. Employee Handbook: Harmony Through Clarity

The rainforest thrives because every organism knows its role in the ecosystem. Similarly, your business flourishes when your team understands expectations, roles, and protocols.

Business Example:
Jane, a boutique owner, struggled with constant employee conflicts—missed shifts, inconsistent customer service, and miscommunication. Frustrated, she created an

employee handbook detailing policies on attendance, dress code, and handling customer disputes. The result? A cohesive team, elevated morale, and a stellar customer experience.

Historical Parallel:

The Roman legions were among the most disciplined military forces in history. Their strict manuals and training protocols ensured every soldier knew their role, which contributed to Rome's dominance. Your business handbook serves the same function—establishing order and consistency.

Takeaway:

A clear employee handbook isn't just a guide—it's a roadmap for teamwork, accountability, and consistency.

2. Health and Safety Policies: Protecting Your People and Business

In the Amazon, survival depends on avoiding hidden dangers like poisonous plants or predators. In business, workplace accidents and unsafe practices are the equivalent risks, threatening not just your team's safety but your company's reputation and finances.

Business Example:

Carlos, the owner of Green Gardens Landscaping, experienced a wake-up call when an employee mishandled equipment, leading to a near-accident. He implemented mandatory safety training, upgraded his protocols, and reduced incidents by 80%. His insurance premiums even dropped as a result.

Historical Parallel:

The construction of the Panama Canal was plagued by disease and dangerous working conditions. Only after implementing strict sanitation and safety measures did the project succeed, showcasing the importance of proactive risk management.

Takeaway:

Health and safety policies aren't optional. They're the foundation of a business that values its people and protects its future.

3. Customer Service Policies: Trust Through Consistency

Just as explorers need a map to navigate dense jungle terrain, your team needs clear customer service protocols to handle interactions with professionalism and care.

Business Example:

Stellar Tech Support faced a PR crisis when a frustrated client's complaint went viral. They responded by implementing a detailed customer service policy: timelines for responses, clear refund guidelines, and follow-up procedures. Complaints dropped, satisfaction soared, and their brand reputation rebounded.

Historical Parallel:

The Ritz-Carlton's legendary customer service standards—where employees are trained to anticipate needs and empowered to solve problems—set the gold standard for hospitality. Their policies create unwavering brand loyalty.

Takeaway:

Clear customer service policies are the compass that ensures every client interaction builds trust and loyalty.

4. Operations and Training Manuals: Your Field Guide to Success

A. Operations Manual – Ensuring Consistency

Like the detailed maps explorers rely on, an operations manual standardizes tasks to ensure consistency and efficiency.

Business Example:

Paula's Pastries faced customer complaints about inconsistent product quality. Paula created an operations manual outlining standardized recipes and processes. The result? Flawless pastries, happy customers, and a smoother workflow.

B. Training Manual – Empowering New Hires

Starting in the jungle without a guide is daunting—and so is onboarding without a training manual. Equip your new hires with a comprehensive guide to ensure they succeed.

Business Example:

Sparkling Clean Services struggled with high turnover until they developed a training eloped a training manual. New hires now hit the ground running, turnover dropped, and customer satisfaction hit record highs.

Historical Parallel:

The McDonald's franchise model thrives on detailed manuals and training programs that ensure a Big Mac tastes the same in New York as it does in Tokyo. Standardization fuels scalability.

Takeaway:

Manuals aren't just for big corporations. They're the foundation of any scalable, consistent business.

5. Legal Safeguards: Protection from Hidden Traps

The Amazon has its share of quicksand and predators. In business, legal troubles can be just as sudden and devastating. Protect your business with these key safeguards:

A. Non-Disclosure Agreements (NDAs): Protect Your Secrets

Whether it's proprietary technology, sensitive client data, or trade secrets, NDAs ensure your intellectual property stays secure.

Business Example:

Tech Innovators required employees and contractors to sign NDAs during a new product launch. The result? Their software launch remained secure, and they beat competitors to market.

B. Vendor Contracts: Clear Expectations, Fewer Surprises

Without vendor contracts, you're vulnerable to missed deadlines or low-quality deliverables.

Business Example:

Urban Greens Market learned this the hard way when a vendor's repeated delays cost them thousands. After implementing vendor contracts with clear terms, accountability improved, and delays became a thing of the past.

Historical Parallel:

The Medici Bank in Renaissance Italy revolutionized banking by introducing contracts that outlined clear expectations, reducing financial disputes and ensuring stability.

Takeaway:

Legal protections are your armor, allowing you to innovate and grow without fear of costly surprises.

Thriving in the Business Jungle

The Amazon teaches us that survival requires strategy, preparation, and adaptability. In business, these qualities translate to robust policies, clear procedures, and legal safeguards.

Business Example:

Andrea's Art Studio faced a wrongful termination lawsuit. Because she had a detailed employee handbook and documented performance reviews, she proved her actions were fair and professional. The case was dismissed, saving her business from financial and reputational ruin.

Takeaway:

Preparation isn't just about preventing crises—it's about building a business that can thrive, no matter the challenge.

Next Stop: The Australian Outback – Harnessing Resources for Financial Mastery

With your policies and procedures in place, it's time to venture into the arid Australian Outback, where survival depends on managing resources wisely. In the next chapter, we'll dive into financial resilience—mastering cash flow, budgeting, and sustainability to ensure your business thrives in even the harshest conditions.

Are you ready to make your finances as unshakable as your vision? Let's crunch the numbers and secure your legacy.

Action Items – Stop #3: Surviving the Amazon Rainforest

To fortify your business against risks and challenges, take these action steps:

1. Establish Clear Policies – Your Business Survival Kit

- **Create or update your Employee Handbook** with policies on attendance, dress code, customer service expectations, and workplace behavior.

- **Develop a Customer Service Policy** outlining response times, refund/exchange guidelines, and escalation procedures.

- **Draft Health & Safety Procedures** to minimize risks and protect your team (e.g., training programs, emergency protocols).

2. Standardize Operations – Ensure Consistency & Efficiency

- **Write an Operations Manual** covering key processes to maintain quality and efficiency.

- **Develop a Training Manual** for new hires to ensure a smooth onboarding process and reduce turnover.

- **Schedule a team training session** to reinforce these policies and answer questions.

3. Strengthen Legal Safeguards – Protect Your Business

- **Implement NDAs (Non-Disclosure Agreements)** for employees, contractors, and partners handling sensitive information.

- **Review and update Vendor Contracts** to ensure clear terms, deadlines, and accountability.

- **Consult a legal expert** (if needed) to ensure your policies and contracts provide maximum protection.

4. Assess and Improve Risk Management

- **Identify the top 3 potential risks** your business faces (e.g., lawsuits, product defects, employee disputes).

- **Create a crisis response plan** to handle unexpected challenges effectively.

- **Review your business insurance** to ensure you're covered for key risks.

5. Commit to Continuous Improvement

- **Set a quarterly review** of your policies and procedures to ensure they remain relevant and effective.

- **Collect feedback from employees and customers** to refine your processes.

- **Stay adaptable**—when challenges arise, adjust and improve your safeguards.

Notes & Reflection

Notes & Reflection

CHAPTER SIX

Stop #4 – Trek the Australian Outback...

WISE USE OF YOUR RESOURCES IS REQUIRED HERE, SO LET'S TAKE A LOOK AT YOUR MONEY AND FINANCES.

"In the middle of difficulty lies opportunity." – Albert Einstein

Stop #4 – Trek the Australian Outback: Mastering Resourcefulness on the Entrepreneurial Journey

The Australian Outback, vast and seemingly barren, is a place where only the resourceful can survive. In the same way, running a business often requires navigating harsh conditions where resources are limited and the terrain is unpredictable. But with the right tools, preparation, and adaptability, even the toughest environments can lead to growth and success.

1. The Income Statement: Your Survival Map

Just like explorers charting a course through the Outback, the income statement offers a map to guide your business. It tells the story of your revenue, expenses, and profitability—essentially, where you've been, where you are, and where you're headed.

Key Elements:

- **Revenue:** Just like finding a waterhole, revenue is the vital resource for your business. It's the fuel that keeps your business alive.

- **Cost of Goods Sold (COGS):** The cost of creating or providing your product or service. It's like your supply of food and water in the Outback—essential for survival.

- **Operating Expenses:** These are the everyday needs—marketing, rent, salaries. Just as a traveler must carefully ration resources, you must manage these costs.

- **Net Income:** What remains after expenses. This is your "profit oasis," the ultimate goal, where your hard work translates into reward.

Example: Sarah, founder of a sustainable clothing brand, noticed a steady decline in her profits. Upon examining her income statement, she discovered her packaging costs were eating into her margins. After sourcing more affordable, eco-friendly materials, she increased profitability while staying true to her sustainable values. By adjusting her income strategy, Sarah not only recovered but positioned her brand for future growth.

Takeaway: Just as a map guides an explorer through the Outback, your income statement helps you navigate your business' profitability and identify areas to optimize.

2. The Cash Flow Statement: Your Lifeblood

Cash flow is the heartbeat of your business, much like water in the Outback. While profitability may indicate success, cash flow ensures you can pay your bills, invest in opportunities, and keep your operations running smoothly. A business with no cash flow, just like an explorer without water, won't survive for long.

Key Components:

- **Operating Activities:** Cash generated from day-to-day business operations. It's like your daily supply of water—you need it consistently to keep going.

- **Investing Activities:** Cash spent on long-term investments such as equipment, technology, or real estate. This is your long-term survival strategy.

- **Financing Activities:** External funds—loans, investments, or equity—that fuel your business. Just like a well-placed resource in the Outback, these help you survive through tough times.

Example: Ben, the owner of a small café, was surprised by his financial struggles despite good sales. A deep dive into his cash flow statement revealed the issue: his cash was tied up in excess inventory. By improving his inventory management and securing quicker payments from customers, Ben was able to free up cash flow and keep his business thriving.

Takeaway: Healthy cash flow is essential for survival and growth. Just like water in the desert, it must be managed carefully to keep your business alive through both calm and challenging times.

3. The Balance Sheet: Your Compass

The balance sheet is like your compass, providing a snapshot of your business' financial health. It shows what you own (assets), what you owe (liabilities), and what's left for you (equity). In the Outback, your compass ensures you're heading in the right direction. For entrepreneurs, your balance sheet guides you in making informed, strategic decisions.

Key Components:

- **Assets:** Everything your business owns—cash, equipment, inventory. These are your survival tools.

- **Liabilities:** What your business owes—loans, supplier payments, taxes. Just like carrying a heavy load in the desert, too many liabilities can weigh you down.

- **Equity:** The difference between what you own and owe. It's the solid foundation beneath your feet, the stake you've built in your business.

Example: Leo, the owner of a construction company, had a strong revenue stream but was burdened by short-term debts. By focusing on paying down liabilities and building cash reserves, Leo improved his balance sheet and created a solid foundation for growth, even attracting potential investors.

Takeaway: A well-managed balance sheet signals strength and stability, enabling you to weather financial storms and pursue opportunities with confidence.

Funding Your Business: Fuel for Growth

In the Outback, finding water can make the difference between life and death. Similarly, securing funding is crucial to your business' survival and growth. Whether through loans, grants, or investments, knowing how to fuel your business is a key part of sustainable growth.

Funding Strategies:

- **Equity Financing:** Offering ownership in exchange for capital. This is ideal for fast-growing businesses looking for major expansion.

- **Debt Financing:** Borrowing money to retain ownership, but carefully planning for repayment. This strategy works well for businesses looking to scale without giving up control.

- **Grants:** Non-repayable funds provided by governments or organizations for mission-aligned businesses. These are perfect for businesses focused on community impact or innovation.

Example: Ava, who ran a small vegan bakery, sought funding to expand her business. With a solid business plan and financial data, she secured a loan that enabled her to open a second location. This strategic funding fueled her growth and allowed her to double both her impact and revenue.

Takeaway: Just as finding water is essential in the Outback, securing funding is crucial for your business' growth. Choose the right funding strategy that aligns with your long-term goals.

Final Thoughts: Thriving in the Outback of Business

The Outback teaches us that success is not about abundance; it's about adaptability and resourcefulness. Entrepreneurs face their own version of the Outback, navigating financial challenges with resilience and strategic thinking. By mastering financial tools like the income statement, cash flow statement, and balance sheet, you can turn a desert into a thriving oasis of opportunity.

Wisdom to Carry Forward:

- **Stay Prepared:** Keep your financial documents up to date, so you can quickly adapt to new challenges and opportunities.

- **Stay Resourceful:** Use what you have wisely and optimize existing resources before seeking more.

- **Stay Strategic:** Use your financial data as a compass to guide your decisions.

As you journey through the entrepreneurial Outback, remember that it's not the abundance of resources that matters, but your ability to maximize them.

Next Stop: Summit Mt. Everest – No One Climbs Alone

With your financial house in order, it's time to focus on what truly elevates your business—building a dream team. As we prepare to scale Mt. Everest, we'll explore how to recruit, inspire, and lead individuals who align with your vision. Because, just as no one climbs Everest alone, no great achievement is accomplished in isolation. Ready to scale new heights? Let's tackle leadership together.

Action Items – Stop #4: Mastering Resourcefulness in the Entrepreneurial Outback

To build financial resilience and make the most of your resources, take these action steps:

1. Get Clear on Your Financial Health

- **Review Your Income Statement** to identify profit margins, unnecessary expenses, and growth opportunities.

- **Analyze Your Cash Flow Statement** to ensure you have enough liquidity to cover operational costs.

- **Evaluate Your Balance Sheet** to understand assets, liabilities, and overall financial stability.

2. Strengthen Cash Flow Management

- **Optimize Accounts Receivable** by invoicing promptly and setting clear payment terms.

- **Negotiate with Vendors** to secure better pricing and flexible payment schedules.

- **Reduce Unnecessary Expenses** by reviewing subscriptions, overhead, and cost-heavy processes.

3. Align Your Funding Strategy with Your Vision

- **Assess Your Business's Funding Needs**—expansion, new hires, equipment, etc.

- **Explore Funding Options** such as small business loans, grants, or investor partnerships.

- **Prepare a Strong Business Plan** with clear financial projections to secure funding.

4. Build a Sustainable Financial System

- **Implement Financial Tracking Tools** (e.g., QuickBooks, Xero, or simple spreadsheets).

- **Schedule Monthly Financial Reviews** to stay proactive in managing your business health.

- **Consult a Financial Advisor** if needed to optimize tax strategies and financial planning.

5. Commit to Financial Discipline & Growth

- **Create a Rainy-Day Fund** to protect your business from unexpected challenges.

- **Set Financial Goals** for revenue, profit margins, and debt reduction.

- **Develop a Long-Term Strategy** for scaling your business sustainably.

Notes & Reflection

Notes & Reflection

CHAPTER SEVEN

Stop #5 – Summit Mt. Everest...

NO ONE HAS EVER SUMMITED ALONE; THERE'S ALWAYS BEEN A TEAM. WHO IS ON YOUR TEAM AND HOW ARE YOU LEADING?

"If you want to go fast, go alone. If you want to go far, go together." – African Proverb

Stop #5 – Summit Mt. Everest: No One Climbs Alone – Building Your Team and Leading

As any seasoned climber knows, reaching the summit of Mt. Everest isn't an individual feat. It takes a team—Sherpas, guides, and fellow climbers—working in unison to tackle the treacherous terrain and overcome the impossible. Similarly, building a business demands teamwork, trust, and leadership. No entrepreneur, no matter how visionary, can scale the heights alone. To truly succeed, you must assemble the right people, lead with purpose, and ensure everyone is aligned and empowered to make the journey together.

Example: Olivia, a founder in the renewable energy space, had a bold vision to revolutionize clean power. But the magnitude of her dream quickly revealed that it was too much for one person to shoulder. She knew she needed a strong team to help turn her vision into reality. By surrounding herself with industry experts, empowering her team to take ownership of key areas, and fostering a culture of trust, Olivia didn't just build a business—she ignited a movement.

This stop on the journey is about assembling your dream team, cultivating leadership, and realizing that the climb is a collective effort. Let's explore how you can create, lead, and empower your "Everest team" to reach new heights together.

1. The Climb Is a Team Effort: Build Your Business Framework

No climber reaches the summit without a clear path, and no business thrives without a solid framework. Think of your organizational structure as the ropes, ladders, and guides that keep everyone connected to the mission, ensuring no one gets lost along the way. Without a clear structure, a business risks inefficiency, confusion, and missed opportunities.

Types of Organizational Structures:
- **Hierarchical:** The traditional model with defined leadership roles and clear chains of command.

  ○ **Pros:** Predictable decision-making and established roles.

- **Cons:** Can stifle innovation and creativity if overly rigid.

- **Flat:** Often used by startups, this structure emphasizes collaboration and autonomy.

  - **Pros:** Encourages agility, flexibility, and creativity.

  - **Cons:** Can lead to role confusion and lack of accountability without clear boundaries.

- **Matrix:** Combines aspects of both hierarchical and flat models, promoting project-based collaboration across teams.

  - **Pros:** Excellent for dynamic, multi-disciplinary teams with shared goals.

  - **Cons:** Requires constant communication to avoid conflicts.

Steps to Design Your Structure:
- **Define Key Roles:** Determine which functions are necessary for your business to thrive—operations, sales, customer service, etc.

- **Clarify Responsibilities:** Ensure each team member knows their specific role and how it ties into the larger mission.

- **Create Visuals:** Use an organizational chart to visually represent roles and connections. This makes the structure clear for everyone.

Example: Nina, founder of a sustainable fashion brand, struggled with managing everything herself as demand grew. By hiring a COO to oversee operations, delegating social media tasks to an agency, and empowering her team, she established a streamlined organizational structure that allowed her to scale her business without sacrificing quality.

Takeaway: Establishing a solid organizational structure is like setting up base camp before tackling the climb—it ensures everyone knows where they stand and how they contribute to the overall mission.

2. Build Your Sherpa Team: Hire for Strengths You Don't Have

No one climbs Everest without Sherpas—local experts who know the terrain, carry heavy loads, and provide guidance. Similarly, you can't lead your business alone. Your leadership team should complement your strengths and fill in the gaps in areas where you might lack expertise.

Key Leadership Roles:

- **CEO:** The visionary leader who keeps the mission at the forefront.

- **CFO:** The financial strategist who ensures resources are invested wisely.

- **COO:** The operations mastermind who creates systems to keep everything running smoothly.

- **CMO:** The marketing expert who crafts the story and attracts the right audience.

- **HR Leader:** The culture builder who ensures the team thrives in a positive, supportive environment.

Tips for Assembling Your Dream Team:

- **Hire Complementary Strengths:** Focus on people who excel in areas where you're weaker.

- **Align on Values:** Skills are important, but shared values and a passion for the mission are non-negotiable.

- **Set Clear Expectations:** Each leader should own their lane and understand how their role drives the overall vision.

Example: Chris, founder of a tech platform focused on mental health, surrounded himself with a strong leadership team. He hired a CFO to secure funding, a COO to scale operations, and a CMO to grow their audience. Together, they turned his vision into a thriving, impactful business that touched countless lives.

Takeaway: Building your Sherpa team is about hiring individuals who not only complement your strengths but share your vision and are committed to your cause.

3. Leadership: Be the Guide Who Inspires and Empowers

A successful leader is not just someone who gives directions, but someone who inspires, empowers, and encourages their team to achieve the impossible. As the head guide of your business, your role is to communicate the vision, foster trust, and create an environment where everyone feels motivated to contribute their best efforts.

Key Leadership Qualities:

- **Vision:** Clearly articulate the mission and the steps needed to achieve it.

- **Empathy:** Understand and respond to the needs and concerns of your team.

- **Adaptability:** Be flexible and ready to adjust to changing circumstances without losing sight of the end goal.

- **Decisiveness:** Make bold decisions, even when the path forward isn't entirely clear.

How to Lead Effectively:

- **Foster open communication:** A true leader listens as much as they speak, ensuring that everyone's voice is heard.

- **Set clear, shared goals:** Ensure everyone is aligned on what the team is working toward.

- **Recognize and celebrate wins:** Take time to celebrate progress, no matter how small, to maintain motivation.

- **Invest in your team's growth:** Provide mentorship, training, and development opportunities for your team members.

Example: Leah, the founder of a social impact nonprofit, saw her team's productivity skyrocket after she prioritized one-on-one mentorship and transparent goal-setting. By investing in her team's development and aligning everyone with a shared vision, Leah created an unstoppable force for good.

Takeaway: Great leadership is about guiding, empowering, and inspiring your team. When your team feels supported and valued, they will work together to overcome challenges and achieve greatness.

4. Expand Your Base Camp: Leverage Outsourcing for Growth

As climbers rely on base camps for support, so too can entrepreneurs rely on outsourcing to handle key tasks and fuel growth. Outsourcing allows you to delegate work that doesn't need to be done in-house, freeing up time and resources to focus on your strengths.

What to Outsource:

- **Admin Tasks:** Payroll, scheduling, or customer service inquiries.

- **Creative Work:** Social media management, graphic design, or branding.

- **Customer Support:** Partner with professionals to provide exceptional client experience.

How to Choose Partners:

- **Do Your Research:** Ensure the outsourcing partner has the expertise and reputation to deliver high-quality work.

- **Define Deliverables:** Be clear about goals, expectations, and timelines to avoid misunderstandings.

- **Monitor and Adjust:** Regularly check in to ensure quality and alignment with your goals.

Example: Sophia, founder of an online education platform, outsourced tasks like video editing and course design to free up time for building partnerships and growing her student base. This allowed her to scale faster and focus on high-value activities.

Takeaway: Just like a base camp supports climbers in their journey, outsourcing allows your business to focus on its core strengths while delegating non-essential tasks to trusted partners.

Final Thought: The Summit Is a Shared Victory

Reaching the summit, whether it's Mt. Everest or your business goal, is never about one person. It's a shared journey built on resilience, trust, and teamwork. When you assemble the right people, lead with purpose, and invest in a supportive, empowering culture, you create a legacy that stands the test of time.

Remember, you're climbing not just for yourself but for the community you serve and the impact you aim to create. Celebrate how far you've come, and prepare for the higher peaks that are yet to be conquered.

Next Stop: A New Horizon – Scaling Beyond the Summit

Once you've reached the summit, the journey continues. Scaling your business beyond the peak requires further expansion, new goals, and innovative approaches. But with the right team and leadership, the next horizon is always within reach. Ready to climb even higher? Let's keep pushing forward.

Action Items – Stop #5: Building Your Dream Team & Leading with Purpose

To summit your entrepreneurial Everest, take these key action steps:

1. Establish Your Business Framework

- **Define Your Organizational Structure** (Hierarchical, Flat, or Matrix) to ensure clarity in roles.

- **Create an Org Chart** to visualize team dynamics and decision-making pathways.

- **Clarify Responsibilities** so each team member understands their contribution to the mission.

2. Build Your Leadership Team

- **Identify Leadership Gaps** and hire for strengths you don't have.

- **Prioritize Values Alignment** when hiring to ensure mission-driven leadership.

- **Set Clear Roles & Expectations** for each leader to own their responsibilities.

3. Develop Your Leadership Style

- **Communicate a Clear Vision** so your team stays aligned with the mission.

- **Foster a Culture of Trust** by being transparent and open to feedback.

- **Recognize & Reward Contributions** to keep motivation high.

- **Invest in Professional Development** to help your team grow alongside your business.

4. Optimize Operations Through Outsourcing

- **Identify Tasks to Outsource** (e.g., admin work, creative tasks, or customer support).

- **Vet Potential Partners** to ensure alignment with your business values.

- **Monitor Outsourced Work** to maintain quality and alignment with goals.

5. Strengthen Team Resilience & Culture

- **Hold Regular Team Check-ins** to maintain alignment and address challenges.

- **Encourage Collaboration** through open communication and shared goals.

- **Create a Supportive Work Environment** that prioritizes well-being and innovation.

Notes & Reflection

Notes & Reflection

CHAPTER EIGHT

Break after completing the 1st Challenge: Business Foundation

"*S uccess is not the key to happiness. Happiness is the key to success. If you love what you are doing, you will be successful.*" — *Albert Schweitzer*

Break After Completing the First Challenge: Building Your Business Foundation

Pause. Reflect. Celebrate.

You've done it! Take a moment to honor this incredible milestone: you've built the foundation for your purpose-driven business. This is your "base camp" moment, where preparation and possibility meet. Like an architect laying the cornerstone of a magnificent structure, you've set the stage for a legacy that will impact generations to come. Building a business isn't just about checking off boxes—it's about crafting something deeply meaningful and creating a vision that resonates far beyond the initial idea.

Every decision you've made so far—every system, strategy, and action—has been an act of courage. You've breathed life into a dream that only you could create. This moment is yours to reflect, acknowledge your wins, and recharge before you continue this monumental journey.

Looking Back: What You've Built So Far

Let's pause to reflect on the key stops you've already navigated on this incredible journey. These milestones have solidified the foundation you need for sustained growth and impact.

Stop #1: The African Savannah – The Heartbeat of Your Business

Your mission, vision, and values are the heartbeat of your business—the compass that guides you through challenges, decisions, and opportunities alike. By aligning your "why" with your work, you've created a business that is rooted in purpose and authenticity.

Real-World Win: Ella, a nutritionist, was initially lost in a saturated market. She struggled to find a unique angle until she narrowed her focus to empowering busy moms to live healthier lives. This clarity allowed her to not only stand out but to connect deeply with a community that resonated with her mission. Her purpose became the driving force behind her brand, helping her build a loyal following and thriving business.

Historical Example: Think of Apple, when Steve Jobs and Steve Wozniak first started the company. Their shared vision was to empower individuals through technology. This clarity became Apple's heartbeat, driving innovation and guiding every product they launched. Their mission has always been at the core of their success.

Stop #2: The Andes Mountains – Big-Picture Thinking

From the high altitudes of the Andes, you've learned to step back and see the bigger picture. Your business strategy became your map—both ambitious and deeply aligned with your purpose. You've shifted from working in your business to working on it.

Real-World Win: Tom, who had been running a small catering business, felt stuck in a cycle of mediocrity. After analyzing his market, he identified an untapped niche in corporate catering. By revamping his strategy to focus on this segment, he was able to triple his revenue in less than a year, demonstrating that clear purpose combined with strategic planning can unlock exponential growth.

Historical Example: Walt Disney's decision to expand from animation to theme parks in the 1950s is an excellent example of big-picture thinking. Disney saw the potential to build a family entertainment empire, far beyond the realm of cartoons. His strategic move revolutionized the entertainment industry and changed the way people experienced storytelling.

Stop #3: The Amazon Rainforest – Protection Through Systems

In the unpredictable Amazon, you've built the essential systems to safeguard your business. Legal protections, operational workflows, and risk management strategies are now your safety nets, ensuring that your business can adapt and thrive, no matter what challenges come your way.

Real-World Win: Lena, who ran an online boutique, faced a major crisis when a supplier delayed shipments for weeks. She was forced to re-think her approach. By implementing contingency contracts and better inventory management systems, Lena not only weathered the storm but turned the situation into an opportunity for increased efficiency and resilience in her business.

Historical Example: During the early 20th century, Ford Motor Company's assembly line revolutionized manufacturing. The systems they implemented to produce cars efficiently and with high quality laid the groundwork for Ford's ongoing success. These systems also protected Ford from the volatility of the early automotive market.

Stop #4: The Australian Outback – Financial Fortitude

In the harsh Australian Outback, you learned to master your finances. Managing cash flow, pricing for profit, and building a sustainable financial model were your tools for navigating this tough landscape. You've laid the groundwork for future growth, creating a financial cushion that will support your business for years to come.

Real-World Win: David, the owner of a gym, struggled with profitability despite a steady influx of clients. After conducting a financial audit, he optimized his expenses and adjusted his pricing model. This not only turned his business around but gave him the financial stability to reinvest in growth.

Historical Example: One of the greatest examples of financial fortitude comes from the rise of Microsoft. In the early 1990s, Bill Gates and Paul Allen made a strategic decision to license Windows to computer manufacturers instead of selling it outright. This financial model gave Microsoft a consistent revenue stream and transformed the company into a dominant force in the tech world.

Stop #5: Mt. Everest – Building Your Dream Team

At the peak of Mt. Everest, you explored the importance of collaboration. Building a team, delegating effectively, and leading with intention have set the stage for growth that's bigger than any solo journey. You've created an environment where your team can scale with you and help you push through new challenges.

Real-World Win: Sophia, a freelance graphic designer, felt overwhelmed by administrative work. By outsourcing her bookkeeping and hiring an assistant to handle client communication, she regained her creative focus and doubled her capacity to take on new clients. With a strong team behind her, her business flourished.

Historical Example: In the early days of Amazon, Jeff Bezos was clear about the need for a strong team to support the company's massive vision. By surrounding himself with talented individuals who shared his passion, Amazon was able to grow from a small online bookstore to the global powerhouse it is today.

Reflecting on the Foundation: Your Guiding Questions

Before you jump into the next phase of growth, take a moment to ask yourself these key questions to ensure your foundation is solid:

- **Does my mission, vision, and values still spark joy and clarity?** Check if your purpose is still aligned with who you are and what you want to achieve.

- **Is my strategy aligned with my long-term goals?** Review your plan and make sure it will lead you to your desired future.

- **Have I built systems that protect my business from unexpected challenges?** Confirm that your systems and processes are resilient and adaptable.

- **Are my finances organized and sustainable for the road ahead?** Ensure that your financial systems are built for both short-term success and long-term sustainability.

- **Do I have the right team in place, and am I leading them with purpose?** Ensure your team's strengths align with your goals, and that you're leading with a clear vision.

If you can answer "yes" to most of these, you're ready for the next chapter. If not, take this time to refine and adjust. Success isn't about perfection; it's about continuous growth and improvement.

Next Challenge: Circle, Marketing, and Sales

Now that your foundation is rock-solid, it's time to amplify your reach and increase your impact. This next phase is about building relationships, telling your brand story, and connecting authentically with your community.

- **Building Your Circle:** Your community is your most valuable asset. These are your customers, advocates, and partners who share your values and believe in your vision. We'll explore how to nurture and grow this tribe.

- **Marketing with Purpose:** Your brand's story is powerful. We'll discuss how to craft content and campaigns that resonate deeply with your audience and inspire action.

- **Sales with Integrity:** Sales isn't just about transactions; it's about building trust and solving problems. We'll explore how to sell confidently and create a sales process that reflects your values.

Take a Break, Recharge, and Prepare for Expansion

Building a business is a marathon, not a sprint. So, before you charge ahead, take this time to celebrate how far you've come. Reflect, recharge, and realign with your vision. The next phase is where your foundation transforms into a true impact. When you're ready, we'll journey to Madagascar—a vibrant landscape that will inspire the growth of your tribe and the amplification of your business.

The adventure is just beginning, and together, we'll make this legacy unforgettable. Keep climbing, and let's build something extraordinary!

Action Items – Base Camp Reflection & Preparation for Growth

You've built a strong foundation—now take a moment to reflect, celebrate, and prepare for the next phase of your journey.

1. Pause & Celebrate Your Wins

- **Reflect on your progress:** Revisit key milestones and acknowledge how far you've come.

- **Recognize your resilience:** Every system, strategy, and decision you've implemented is a testament to your commitment.

- **Celebrate small and big victories:** Treat yourself—whether it's a day off, a small reward, or simply acknowledging your efforts.

2. Evaluate & Strengthen Your Foundation

- **Review your mission, vision, and values:** Do they still align with your purpose?

- **Assess your strategy:** Ensure your long-term goals remain clear and actionable.

- **Check your business systems:** Identify gaps in workflows, legal protections, or operational efficiency.

- **Analyze your finances:** Confirm that your pricing, cash flow, and profitability are on track.

- **Evaluate your team:** Are the right people in place, and are you leading effectively?

3. Make Adjustments for a Stronger Future

- **Refine any misaligned areas**—whether it's your strategy, finances, or team structure.

- **Strengthen weak points** to ensure smoother operations as you scale.

- **Seek feedback** from mentors, peers, or your team for fresh insights.

4. Recharge Before Scaling

- **Take a short break** to reset and gain fresh energy for the next phase.

- **Reconnect with your 'why'**—this will fuel your passion for growth.

- **Visualize your next level** and get excited about expanding your reach.

5. Get Ready for Expansion: Marketing & Sales

- **Build your community:** Identify ways to grow and engage your audience authentically.

- **Strengthen your brand messaging:** Ensure clarity in your marketing to attract your ideal clients.

- **Refine your sales approach:** Shift from selling to serving—solve problems and create value.

Notes & Reflection

Notes & Reflection

CHAPTER NINE

Stop #6 – Enjoy the stunning tapestry of diversity in Madagascar...

THE UNIQUENESS OF THE ENVIRONMENT AND WILDLIFE WILL LEAD YOU TO YOUR CIRCLE.

"Alone, we can do so little; together, we can do so much." – Helen Keller

Stop #6 – The Stunning Tapestry of Madagascar: Finding Your Circle

Imagine standing in the vivid, life-filled landscapes of Madagascar. The island pulses with life—an intricate tapestry where each creature, plant, and natural element has its place. From the playful lemurs leaping between trees to the kaleidoscope of chameleons blending seamlessly with their surroundings, every being adapts and contributes to the ecosystem. Much like this natural harmony, your business flourishes when you find your circle—the community of people who don't just buy from you, but who champion your mission and embody your purpose.

Your circle isn't simply a customer base—it's a collection of relationships that power your business. A thriving circle is more than transactional; it's about creating connections with people who share your values, who grow alongside you, and who will carry your legacy into the world. Building your circle is not only about expanding your influence; it's about deepening the impact of your business.

1. Who's in Your Circle? Identifying Your Ideal Client

Your ideal client is the heartbeat of your business—much like how Madagascar is home to unique species, your circle is filled with individuals uniquely aligned with your mission. Identifying them means understanding who they are, what they care about, and how they think and feel. Here's how you can define your ideal client:

Crafting Your Ideal Client Profile:
- **Demographics**: These are the basic characteristics that define your ideal client.

  - *Example*: "Eco-conscious women aged 30-50 who prioritize sustainable products and live in urban areas."

- **Psychographics**: What motivates them? What do they value most?

  - *Example*: "They are passionate about environmental stewardship, value authenticity, and seek simplicity in their lifestyle."

- **Pain Points**: What problems are they trying to solve, and how can you help?

- *Example*: "They struggle to find stylish, high-quality, yet affordable eco-friendly products."

- **Buying Habits**: What behaviors do they exhibit when making a purchase?

  - *Example*: "They research brands deeply, seeking reviews and transparency before making a decision."

Real-World Example: Persona:

Name: Mia Torres

Age: 36

Passion: Ethical and sustainable living

Need: Accessible, stylish, eco-conscious lifestyle products

Challenge: Balancing her values with affordability and convenience

By clearly defining your ideal client, you create a map to help guide every action and decision in your business. You're no longer guessing what your audience wants—you know exactly how to connect with them and meet their needs.

2. Building Your Circle: The Power of Community

Your circle is your lifeline. It's not just a transactional relationship; it's a network of people who believe in your mission, values, and purpose. A thriving community isn't built overnight, but when nurtured with care and intention, it becomes the most valuable part of your business. Let's explore the pillars of a strong community:

The Pillars of a Strong Community:

- **Shared Values**: People want to support brands that reflect their beliefs and principles.

  - *Example*: "Our community values sustainability, reducing waste, supporting artisans, and fostering a lifestyle of intentional living."

- **Emotional Connection**: Loyalty is built when people feel heard, seen, and valued.

  - *Example*: "Every purchase is more than just a product—it's a step towards a shared vision of conscious living."

- **Advocacy and Loyalty**: True loyalty means your circle becomes your most powerful advocate.

  - *Example*: "Our loyal customers spread the word about our mission and products, helping us grow organically."

A business with a strong, emotionally connected community doesn't need to compete for attention. The community does the work for you, advocating and promoting your brand in a way that feels authentic and natural.

3. How to Attract and Grow Your Circle

Your circle is already out there—you simply need to draw them in. The best way to do this is with authenticity and consistency. It's not just about reaching as many people as possible; it's about connecting with the right people and inviting them into your world.

Ways to Attract Your Circle:

- **Tell Your Story**: People connect with stories, not just products. Share the journey of your business, why you started, and the mission you're on.

  - *Example*: "We started with a belief that sustainability shouldn't come at the expense of style or quality. Our mission is to make eco-friendly living accessible to everyone."

- **Be Relatable**: Speak to your audience as humans, not customers. Build trust and intimacy by showing that you understand their needs and values.

  - *Example*: "We're on this journey with you, one mindful step at a time, and we're here to make this journey a little easier."

- **Engage Actively**: Create meaningful interactions by listening, responding, and participating.

  - *Example*: "We love seeing how you use our products. Tag us to be featured and inspire others!"

Your circle will only grow if you continually engage with your audience in an authentic way. Consistency in communication and involvement makes your brand feel alive and connected.

4. Listening to Your Circle: Evolving with Their Needs

Building a loyal community starts with listening. As your business grows, so will your audience's needs and expectations. Stay attuned to their feedback, desires, and values, and evolve with them.

What They Want:

- **Authenticity and Transparency**: Today's consumers value honesty above all. Show your process, challenges, and triumphs.

  - *Example*: "Every product we create is rooted in transparency—ethical sourcing, sustainable practices, and people-first values."

- **Genuine Connection**: Your community wants to feel like they're part of something bigger. Foster that feeling.

  - *Example*: "When you join us, you're not just buying a product—you're fueling a movement."

Your business becomes not just a transaction, but a cause—something your customers feel personally invested in.

5. Case Study: Lara's Jewelry Collective

Lara, the founder of an ethical jewelry line, struggled at first to stand out in a crowded marketplace. She could have chased the latest trends, but instead, she chose to focus on her mission: creating sustainable, handcrafted jewelry that told a story.

By authentically sharing her creative process on social media, Lara invited her community to get involved by voting on new designs and learning about the artisans behind her pieces. She shared stories, not just of her products, but of the people who made them. Over time, her community grew organically, drawn not only by her products but by the emotional connection they felt to her values.

Today, Lara's jewelry line isn't just about accessories—it's a movement for slow fashion, ethical production, and mindful living. The sense of community she fostered is the heart of her business, helping it thrive in a competitive market.

6. The Next Phase: Expanding Beyond Your Circle

Now that you've built a thriving community, it's time to scale your impact. Think of your brand as a lighthouse, drawing others in with its beacon of purpose. The next phase is all about amplifying your message and reaching more people, while keeping your core mission intact.

In the next chapter, we'll focus on marketing and sales—strategies that will help you grow your influence, increase your revenue, and attract even more followers. But remember, the foundation of this growth will always be the deep, authentic connections you've built with your circle.

Madagascar teaches us that diversity, balance, and intentional growth are the keys to thriving ecosystems—and thriving businesses. As you nurture your circle, remember: it's not about numbers—it's about people. It's about purpose. And it's about the legacy you're creating. Keep building, stay connected, and let your mission lead the way.

Action Items – Building & Nurturing Your Circle

You've identified your ideal client and started building a thriving community—now, let's solidify your next steps.

1. Define & Refine Your Ideal Client

- **Review your ideal client profile**—does it still align with your mission and values?

- **Clarify their biggest challenges, needs, and desires**—are you addressing them effectively?

- **Update your messaging** to ensure it speaks directly to their hearts.

2. Strengthen Your Community with Purpose

- **Foster shared values**—clearly communicate what your brand stands for.

- **Deepen emotional connections**—engage with your audience in meaningful ways.

- **Encourage advocacy**—make it easy and rewarding for your community to share your mission.

3. Expand & Engage Your Circle

- **Share your story authentically**—let people connect with the heart behind your brand.

- **Create interactive content**—polls, Q&A sessions, behind-the-scenes glimpses.

- **Showcase user-generated content**—highlight testimonials and customer experiences.

4. Listen & Adapt to Your Community

- **Actively gather feedback** through surveys, social media, and conversations.

- **Adapt your offerings** based on your audience's evolving needs.

- **Stay transparent**—share your journey, challenges, and wins openly.

5. Prepare for Expansion

- **Identify opportunities to scale your reach**—collaborations, partnerships, or new platforms.

- **Develop a marketing strategy that feels natural**—one that amplifies your mission without compromising authenticity.

- **Align your sales approach with trust and integrity**—focus on serving, not just selling.

Notes & Reflection

Notes & Reflection

CHAPTER TEN

Stop #7 – Deep sea fishing...

HOW WILL YOU ATTRACT YOUR CUSTOMERS?

"Give me a place to stand, and I will move the earth." — Archimedes

Stop #7 – Deep-Sea Fishing: How Will You Attract Your Customers?

Imagine standing at the helm of your boat, the ocean stretching before you. Beneath the waves lies a vibrant ecosystem, teeming with opportunities. But in this vast expanse, success doesn't come by accident—it's intentional. Deep-sea fishing requires skill: choosing the right bait, casting your line in the right place, and knowing exactly which fish you're after. The same is true for marketing.

In marketing, it's not about casting a wide net and hoping for anything to stick. It's about clarity, focus, and purpose. You're not trying to catch every fish in the sea; you're aiming to connect with the right ones. Let's dive into this chapter and craft intentional strategies that will build meaningful relationships, anchor your marketing in authenticity, and keep you on course, even as distractions emerge. Ready to reel in the right catch? Let's dive in.

1. Casting the Right Net: Attracting Your Ideal Customers

In deep-sea fishing, the fish you're targeting determines the bait and gear you use. The same principle applies to marketing: your success depends on knowing your audience deeply and tailoring your efforts to meet them where they are. Let's break down how to hook the right customers.

Steps to Hook the Right Customers:

- **Know Your Target Fish (Audience)**: Each "fish" in the sea has its own preferences, habits, and behaviors. Similarly, your audience is unique, and you need to understand where they "swim" and what they care about.

  - *Example*: If you're selling eco-friendly outdoor gear, you'll want to target eco-conscious adventurers by promoting your brand on nature blogs, sustainability forums, and green lifestyle platforms where your audience spends time.

- **Choose the Right Bait (Messaging)**: The bait you use should speak to your audience's dreams, struggles, and values. Your message needs to resonate with what matters most to them.

- *Example*: For outdoor gear, emphasize how your products allow adventurers to explore the great outdoors without compromising the environment.

- **Use the Right Fishing Gear (Channels)**: Just as you wouldn't use the same tools for catching all fish, you need to meet your audience where they are. Whether they spend time on Instagram, podcasts, or in person, find the best channels to connect with them.

  - *Example*: If your audience loves visual storytelling, platforms like Instagram and TikTok are ideal. If they prefer deeper, more thoughtful content, focus on blogs or email newsletters.

- **Be Patient and Persistent (Building Trust)**: Like fishing, marketing takes time. Building trust with your audience is a long-term effort that requires consistency and value.

  - *Example*: Share weekly behind-the-scenes videos, customer stories, or educational content to keep your audience engaged and invested in your journey.

2. Building Your Personal Brand: Anchor Your Authenticity

Your personal brand is your compass, guiding every action you take. In a sea of distractions, your authenticity becomes the anchor that keeps you steady. Customers don't just buy products—they invest in the story, values, and mission behind your brand.

Why Personal Branding Matters:

- **Stay True to Your Values**: Never compromise your principles for quick wins. Your integrity is your greatest asset, and your audience will value you for staying true to what you believe.

  - *Example*: If sustainability is your mission, resist the temptation to collaborate with fast-fashion brands, even if they promise immediate returns. Stay committed to the principles you stand for.

- **Be Consistent, Not Trendy**: Trends come and go, but a strong, consistent brand endures. Stick to a steady rhythm of messaging that reflects your mission and values.

  - *Example*: Instead of jumping on every viral challenge, create content that educates your audience about your craft, your impact, or your brand story, all while staying aligned with your mission.

- **Build Trust Through Transparency**: People want to connect with what's real. Share your story—the triumphs, the setbacks, and the work that goes into building your brand.

  - *Example*: Post an honest account of your journey to source ethical materials or share a video showing how your team problem-solves challenges.

3. The Long Game: Marketing with Consistency

Deep-sea fishing is a long game. It requires endurance, strategy, and refining your approach as you go. Similarly, marketing success comes from playing the long game. It's about being persistent, staying focused on your goals, and consistently delivering value.

Keys to Playing the Long Game:

- **Stick to a Schedule**: Your audience thrives on reliability. Set a consistent schedule for content creation and stick to it, so your audience knows what to expect and when.

  - *Example*: Commit to posting on Instagram three times a week or sending a monthly "Behind the Brand" email. The regularity builds anticipation and trust.

- **Track, Analyze, and Adapt**: Just as skilled anglers keep logs, tracking your marketing performance is crucial. Review what's working, what isn't, and adapt accordingly.

- *Example*: If video content generates twice the engagement of static posts, prioritize producing more videos and shift resources accordingly.

- **Resist the Shiny Objects**: New trends will always emerge, but not all of them will be right for your audience. Stick to what resonates with your unique community.

  - *Example*: If your audience isn't active on TikTok, don't force a presence there. Focus on the platforms where you already have an engaged audience and content that aligns with their interests.

4. Relationship-Building Tools: CRM as Your Fishing Log

A skilled angler keeps a logbook of every trip, noting the conditions, baits used, and results. In marketing, a Customer Relationship Management (CRM) system is your logbook. It helps you deepen relationships, track customer interactions, and improve your marketing strategies.

How CRM Boosts Your Marketing:

- **Personalized Messaging**: Use data to personalize your interactions with customers, making them feel seen and valued.

  - *Example*: Send a personalized thank-you email after a purchase, including tailored product recommendations based on their preferences or past purchases.

- **Celebrate Milestones**: Celebrate your customers' milestones with them. Whether it's their birthday, an anniversary with your brand, or a significant achievement, make them feel special.

  - *Example*: Offer a discount or a free gift for customers celebrating their first year with your brand.

- **Identify Patterns for Better Decisions**: Use CRM data to spot trends and refine your marketing strategy.

- *Example*: If you notice a surge in interest for a particular product, you can launch a complementary item or create a campaign to highlight that product.

5. Business Examples: Marketing in Action

Sophie's Handmade Jewelry: Sophie's authenticity on Instagram, where she shared her design process and the stories behind her pieces, fueled organic growth. By being transparent about her materials and values, she built trust with her audience, leading to increased loyalty and sales.

Liam's Sustainable Fashion: Liam stood out in the crowded fashion market by sharing honest, behind-the-scenes videos about his eco-friendly production process. His transparency and commitment to sustainable practices helped him build a dedicated following who admired his values and rooted for his success.

Emily's Artisanal Coffee Shop: Emily used her CRM to send personalized drink recommendations to customers based on their preferences, creating a sense of personal connection. This led to higher customer retention and more frequent visits, as customers felt seen and valued by her brand.

Final Thoughts: Navigating the Ocean of Marketing

Deep-sea fishing, and by extension marketing, isn't about casting a net and hoping for the best. It's about precision, strategy, and consistency. When you stay true to your values, engage authentically with your audience, and play the long game, you'll attract more than just customers—you'll cultivate a community of believers in your mission.

As we prepare to move into the next chapter, we'll explore the vibrant coral reefs of customer experience—an ecosystem where businesses rooted in value create ripples of impact that last. Let's dive deep and make waves, creating experiences that turn customers into loyal advocates.

Action Items – Mastering Intentional Marketing

You've cast your line—now it's time to refine your marketing strategy and ensure you're attracting the right audience with purpose and authenticity.

1. Define Your Ideal Customer & Tailor Your Strategy

- **Clarify who you're trying to attract**—refine your ideal customer profile based on their needs, habits, and values.

- **Identify the right platforms**—determine where your audience "swims" and focus your efforts there.

- **Craft compelling messaging**—ensure your content speaks directly to their desires and pain points.

2. Strengthen Your Personal Brand & Stand Out Authentically

- **Stay true to your values**—align all marketing efforts with your mission and avoid distractions that dilute your authenticity.

- **Maintain a consistent voice & presence**—develop a recognizable tone and visual identity across all platforms.

- **Share your journey transparently**—show the behind-the-scenes of your business, including challenges and victories.

3. Commit to Consistency & Long-Term Marketing Success

- **Create a content calendar**—schedule posts, emails, and campaigns to maintain regular engagement.

- **Analyze and refine**—track which strategies work best and adapt your efforts accordingly.

- **Avoid the shiny object syndrome**—stick with proven methods that resonate with your audience instead of chasing fleeting trends.

4. Utilize Relationship-Building Tools (CRM & Engagement Strategies)

- **Leverage a CRM to track and personalize customer interactions.**

- **Celebrate customer milestones**—send personalized messages, discounts, or special offers to build loyalty.

- **Use insights to improve marketing**—monitor engagement patterns to refine your outreach strategy.

5. Apply Lessons from Real-World Examples

- **Identify one business case study that resonates with you** and implement a similar strategy.

- **Experiment with storytelling marketing**—try sharing your process, customer experiences, or impact-driven initiatives.

- **Engage with your audience regularly**—respond to comments, emails, and messages to nurture genuine connections.

Notes & Reflection

Notes & Reflection

CHAPTER ELEVEN

Stop #8 – Savor the abundance of coral reefs...

NOW THAT YOU HAVE YOUR CUSTOMERS, HOW WILL YOU BRING ABOUT VALUE FOR ALL OF YOU?

"Do what you love, and success will follow. Passion is the fuel that turns dreams into reality."
– Unknown

Stop #8 — Savor the Abundance of Coral Reefs: Bringing Value to Your Customers

Imagine diving into a vibrant coral reef, alive with color and movement. This is an ecosystem where every species thrives because the reef provides the right conditions: nourishment, protection, and support. Your business should feel like that reef to your customers—an ecosystem where they are not just satisfied but inspired to stay, grow, and advocate for your brand.

After you've captured your customers' attention, the real challenge is turning transactional interactions into transformational experiences. The key is consistent, undeniable value that keeps them coming back and fosters lasting loyalty. Let's explore how to create your own thriving coral reef of customer relationships—one that nurtures growth for both them and your business.

1. Providing Value: The Heartbeat of Loyalty

Just as a coral reef provides life, shelter, and connection, your business must deliver consistent, meaningful value to sustain long-term relationships with customers. Value is the foundation of loyalty, and your efforts should go beyond simple transactions.

How to Define Value for Your Customers:

- **Consistency is Queen**: A coral reef sustains life day after day, and your business must be just as reliable in providing exceptional quality and experiences.

  - *Example*: A personal trainer might offer weekly, value-packed emails that include actionable workout tips, meal prep guides, and motivational content tailored to clients' needs. These resources keep customers engaged, building trust and long-term loyalty.

- **Surprise & Delight**: Coral reefs are full of hidden treasures, and your business can bring unexpected joy to your customers in the same way. When customers are surprised by thoughtful gestures, they are more likely to become repeat buyers and advocates.

- *Example*: An artisanal candle company might include mini sample scents in each order. This small gesture not only delights customers but encourages them to explore more products, sparking curiosity and repeat purchases.

- **Personalization Creates Connection**: Just as coral reefs adapt to nurture different marine species, your business should personalize interactions to make customers feel recognized and understood. Tailor your services or products to meet the specific needs of each customer.

  - *Example*: A wellness coach might create individualized fitness plans or wellness journeys that cater to each client's unique goals, preferences, and challenges. Every session feels personal and impactful, fostering a deeper emotional connection.

- **Engagement Builds Trust**: Just as marine life depends on vibrant coral reefs, customer relationships grow when nurtured. Keeping customers engaged with meaningful content and interactions builds trust and keeps them loyal.

  - *Example*: A podcast host may offer free, interactive workshops for listeners, or host live Q&A sessions, deepening connections and offering ongoing value that goes beyond the podcast itself.

2. Building Loyalty: Creating a Safe Harbor

Coral reefs offer stability and protection to marine life, and similarly, loyal customers need a sense of security and community. To cultivate loyalty, create a business ecosystem that customers see as a safe harbor—a place where they belong and can thrive.

Strategies to Cultivate Loyalty:

- **Celebrate Customers as Heroes**: Highlight your customers' achievements to make them feel appreciated and part of a community.

  - *Example*: A craft store might showcase customers' creations on social media, tagging them and celebrating their talents. This recognition fosters a sense of pride and belonging, strengthening the emotional bond between the brand

and its customers.

- **Reward Loyalty Thoughtfully**: A rewards program can incentivize customers to return, while showing them they are valued. Design a program that feels meaningful rather than transactional.

  - *Example*: A natural skincare brand might offer a point-based system where customers earn rewards like exclusive products, discounts, or early access to new items. This reinforces their importance to the brand, making them feel like part of an exclusive community.

- **Offer Meaningful Communication**: Show genuine care for your customers' needs by regularly checking in with personalized messages or updates.

  - *Example*: A tech platform might send tailored tips and feature updates based on the tools and services customers use most often. This ongoing, personalized communication helps keep customers engaged and invested in the brand.

3. Encouraging Referrals: Expanding Your Ecosystem

A healthy coral reef naturally attracts new life, and your satisfied customers can do the same for your business. Referrals are an authentic, low-cost way to grow your customer base. By creating an environment where customers feel valued, you make it easy and rewarding for them to spread the word.

How to Spark Organic Referrals:

- **Make Sharing Rewarding**: Incentivize both referrers and their friends to spread the word about your brand.

  - *Example*: A pet care brand could offer a 10% discount to both the person referring and the new customer when they make their first purchase. This mutual benefit encourages existing customers to advocate for the brand while attracting new clients.

- **Simplify the Process**: Make it easy for customers to share your brand by providing shareable links, unique codes, or pre-made templates.

  - *Example*: A language-learning app could encourage users to share their progress certificates on social media by embedding referral codes directly into the certificates, making the referral process seamless.

- **Publicly Acknowledge Your Advocates**: When someone goes out of their way to refer your brand, show appreciation by recognizing their efforts publicly.

  - *Example*: A café might feature the "Customer of the Month" on a board, showcasing their favorite drink or snack, and thanking them for referring new customers. Public recognition makes customers feel valued and strengthens loyalty.

4. Gathering Feedback: Listening to Your Reef

Coral reefs are dynamic ecosystems that adapt to environmental changes. Your business, too, should remain agile, continuously improving based on customer feedback. Actively seeking input and listening to your customers is essential for long-term growth.

Why Feedback Fuels Growth:

- **It Shows You Care**: Asking for feedback demonstrates that you care about your customers' experiences and are committed to meeting their needs.

  - *Example*: A subscription box service could include a QR code with each package, linking to a survey where customers can provide feedback. In exchange for their time, customers receive a 10% discount on their next purchase. This gesture not only shows appreciation but helps the business improve.

- **It Drives Innovation**: Feedback can often reveal untapped opportunities for improvement or new product ideas. By staying open to customer suggestions, you can keep your offerings fresh and relevant.

- *Example*: A coworking space could introduce late-night hours after surveys show that many members are night owls, ensuring their needs are met while growing the business.

- **It Builds Trust**: Transparency in how you act on feedback builds trust. Share what you've learned and how it's leading to improvements in your products or services.

  - *Example*: A boutique gym might openly share survey results with members and communicate how new classes or equipment were introduced based on their feedback. This shows customers that their voices truly influence the brand.

5. Expressing Gratitude: Sustaining the Connection

Just as coral reefs provide constant support to marine life, your business should give more than it takes. By showing gratitude, you nurture customer relationships and build a strong foundation for long-term loyalty.

Creative Ways to Show Gratitude:

- **Unexpected Gifts**: Small surprises can turn a routine experience into something memorable.

  - *Example*: A plant shop could include a care guide and a free sample of plant food with each order. This gesture makes customers feel special and appreciated, encouraging repeat business.

- **Celebrate Customer Milestones**: Recognize and celebrate important moments in your customers' lives, reinforcing the emotional connection with your brand.

  - *Example*: A yoga studio might offer a free class to members who celebrate their one-year membership anniversary. This personalized recognition shows you value their loyalty and investment in your brand.

- **Add Personal Touches**: Thoughtful, personalized touches can make all the difference in building strong relationships.

  - *Example*: An online artisan market could send handwritten thank-you notes, personalized to the specific items customers ordered. This personal touch makes customers feel seen and valued, fostering a deeper connection.

Final Thoughts: Flourish Together

Just like a thriving coral reef, your business can be a place of abundance—a space where customers feel valued, supported, and inspired to stay. By focusing on providing consistent value, cultivating loyalty, encouraging referrals, gathering feedback, and showing gratitude, you can build an ecosystem that thrives not only for your business but also for your customers.

When customers feel they are part of something bigger, they won't just make a transaction—they'll build a lasting relationship with your brand. Together, you'll create a community rooted in trust, authenticity, and shared purpose.

As we move forward, we'll explore how to build sustainability into your business operations. Just like the most resilient coral reefs, your business needs a foundation that lasts for generations. Let's make waves and ensure your legacy endures.

Action Items – Cultivating an Ecosystem of Value & Loyalty

Transform your business into a thriving coral reef—an ecosystem where customers feel valued, connected, and inspired to stay. Use these action steps to build lasting relationships and sustainable success.

1. Provide Undeniable Value

- **Ensure consistency**—deliver high-quality products, services, and content on a regular basis.

- **Create surprise & delight moments**—find small, unexpected ways to add value to each customer interaction.

- **Personalize experiences**—use customer data to offer tailored recommendations or experiences.

- **Engage regularly**—host Q&A sessions, behind-the-scenes content, or interactive events to build trust.

2. Build Loyalty & A Sense of Belonging

- **Celebrate customer achievements**—showcase their success stories and tag them on social media.

- **Develop a thoughtful rewards program**—offer meaningful perks for repeat business.

- **Maintain genuine communication**—send personalized check-ins, appreciation emails, and helpful tips.

3. Encourage Referrals & Word-of-Mouth Growth

- **Implement a referral incentive**—reward both existing and new customers when they spread the word.

- **Make sharing effortless**—provide easy-to-use referral links or pre-made social media templates.

- **Recognize brand advocates**—publicly thank customers who refer others, featuring them in your community.

4. Gather & Act on Customer Feedback

- **Create multiple feedback channels**—use surveys, polls, and direct conversations to gather insights.

- **Analyze & adapt**—identify trends in feedback and implement improvements.

- **Share the results**—let customers know how their feedback shaped new products, services, or policies.

5. Show Genuine Gratitude & Deepen Connections

- **Surprise customers with unexpected gifts**—small tokens of appreciation can make a lasting impact.

- **Celebrate milestones**—acknowledge anniversaries, birthdays, or long-term loyalty with special offers.

- **Add personal touches**—send handwritten notes, voice messages, or personalized emails to express gratitude.

Notes & Reflection

Notes & Reflection

CHAPTER TWELVE

Break after completing the 2nd Challenge: Circle, Marketing, and Sales

"Success is not the result of spontaneous combustion. You must set yourself on fire." – Arnold H. Glasow

Break After Completing the 2nd Challenge: Your Circle, Marketing, and Sales

Congratulations on completing a major milestone in your entrepreneurial journey! You've just navigated the essential work of building your circle, refining your marketing, and mastering sales. This phase was about forming genuine connections, sharpening your message, and offering value that resonates with your audience. Reflect on how far you've come—relationships built, strategies executed, and the impact you've made so far. Now, it's time to celebrate your progress and recharge for what's next.

But let's not stop here. Your journey is far from over. The next phase isn't about doing more; it's about fueling **you**—your energy, mindset, and wellness. These will be the foundation for sustaining your mission and scaling your legacy.

Stop #6 – Explore the Stunning Tapestry of Madagascar: Finding Your Circle

Madagascar is home to an incredibly diverse array of species that thrive because of their interdependent relationships. Your business should operate in the same way—thriving through the interconnectedness of relationships with those who believe in your mission and align with your vision.

Building your circle isn't about trying to be everything to everyone; it's about attracting those who resonate with your values and who feel seen by your work. Your circle is your support system, and cultivating it intentionally ensures that you surround yourself with people who inspire, support, and push you toward your mission.

Real-Life Example:

Maria, a yoga instructor, once struggled in a sea of competition, offering generic classes that failed to stand out. After shifting her focus to a specific niche—stressed professionals craving mindfulness and balance—she transformed her offerings. She started designing lunchtime mindfulness sessions and offering bite-sized meditation sessions online. This shift not only attracted more of her ideal customers but created a loyal community that spoke about her expertise and helped her grow her circle exponentially.

Stop #7 – Deep Sea Fishing: Attracting the Right Customers

The ocean is vast, and while it's full of potential, not every fish is your ideal catch. Deep-sea fishing requires strategy, precision, and the right tools. Similarly, your marketing efforts should be focused on finding your specific audience, speaking to their needs, and offering something irresistible. Marketing isn't about casting a wide net—it's about showing up where your audience is, communicating in a way that speaks to their desires, and offering solutions that meet their needs.

Real-Life Example:

Josh, a café owner, had been stuck relying on walk-ins, but he wanted to attract a more loyal customer base. Instead of using traditional marketing tactics, he created a "Coffee & Community" series that celebrated local culture with art shows, live music, and storytelling nights. The series gave the community a reason to come together at his café. Customers turned into loyal advocates, helping Josh not only retain his current audience but expand it with newcomers who felt drawn to the sense of belonging his café offered.

Stop #8 – Savor the Abundance of Coral Reefs: Delivering Value

Coral reefs are ecosystems of abundance, nurturing life in perfect harmony. Similarly, your business should create an environment where customers feel valued, supported, and connected to something bigger than just a product or service. Delivering value isn't just about meeting customer expectations; it's about creating transformative experiences that turn customers into loyal advocates.

Real-Life Example:

Samantha, a freelance graphic designer, decided to elevate her service offering by not just delivering design projects but also offering ongoing follow-up consultations and design audits. By showing she was invested in her clients' success beyond a single project, Samantha's clients became loyal supporters. They not only stuck around but referred her services to others because of her above-and-beyond service.

Celebrate the Wins

You've laid a strong foundation for your purpose-driven business by building your circle, refining your marketing, and mastering sales strategies. Celebrate the progress you've made and take pride in the relationships you've built. Every connection and strategy executed is a testament to your authenticity, resilience, and commitment to your mission.

Looking Ahead: Energy, Wellness, and Mindset

The next chapter isn't just about external growth—it's about fueling **you**. Your energy, mindset, and wellness are essential to the sustainability of your mission. This phase is about ensuring you have the mental clarity, emotional resilience, and physical vitality to overcome any challenge that comes your way.

Think of this stage as finding your oasis in the desert—a space where you can recharge, recalibrate, and realign with your purpose. By prioritizing your health, creativity, and well-being, you'll be better equipped to continue making an impact and scaling your legacy.

Action Items for This Chapter:

1. Define Your Ideal Customer:

- Who are they? What are their pain points, desires, and challenges?

- What keeps them awake at night, and how can you solve it?

- *Action*: Create a customer avatar with detailed descriptions of their needs, behaviors, and aspirations.

2. Speak Their Language:

- How can you create a conversation that resonates with their concerns and dreams?

- *Action*: Refine your messaging to feel like a personal conversation, one that makes your ideal customer feel heard and understood.

3. Create Safe Spaces:

- Build community spaces—whether online (like Facebook groups or private Slack channels) or offline (in-person meetups, workshops, or events)—where people who resonate with your mission can connect.

- *Action*: Launch an online group for your ideal customers to discuss shared interests, and host monthly virtual or in-person meetups.

4. Show Up Authentically:

- Let your true brand personality shine. This will naturally attract those who resonate with your values.

- *Action*: Post authentic content that reflects your mission, share behind-the-scenes glimpses of your journey, and engage in meaningful conversations on social media or through other marketing channels.

5. Collaborate for Visibility:

○ Partner with like-minded businesses or creators to cross-promote and expand your reach.

○ *Action*: Identify one or two brands or individuals who share a similar audience and collaborate on a product, event, or content series that will introduce your brand to a wider audience.

6. Tell a Story They'll Remember:

○ People don't just buy products—they buy stories that resonate with their own. Share your story and the story of your brand.

○ *Action*: Craft a compelling brand story and weave it into your marketing. Share how you started, the struggles you've faced, and the impact you hope to make through your business.

7. Exceed Expectations:

○ Go above and beyond to surprise and delight your customers.

○ *Action*: Think of one small, thoughtful surprise or gesture you can include in every transaction that will leave a lasting impression on your customers.

8. Build Connection:

○ Your goal is to create an experience, not just a transaction. Make your customers feel seen, heard, and appreciated.

○ *Action*: Engage with your customers after the sale—whether through thank-you notes, follow-up emails, or offering additional resources that help them get the most out of your product or service.

9. Adapt and Innovate:

○ Continuously seek feedback from your customers and use it to improve your offerings.

- *Action*: Set up a feedback system (surveys, direct messages, or informal conversations) and commit to regularly improving based on their input.

Notes & Reflection

Notes & Reflection

CHAPTER THIRTEEN

Stop #9 – Find an oasis in the Sahara Desert...

KNOWING WHEN AND WHERE TO SPEND OR CONSERVE YOUR ENERGY IS KEY TO MAKING IT TO AN OASIS.

"Almost everything will work again if you unplug it for a few minutes, including you." –
Anne Lamott

Stop #9 – Find an Oasis in the Sahara Desert: Mastering Energy Management

Imagine standing in the heart of the Sahara, where the sun blazes mercilessly, and the horizon feels infinite. Every step requires intention—each decision could mean the difference between finding shade or running out of steam. Your entrepreneurial journey is no different. Success doesn't come from endless hustle but from knowing when to push forward and when to pause, recalibrate, and refuel.

This chapter is about **energy mastery**: learning when to conserve your strength, where to direct it, and how to sustain yourself for the long haul. In the desert of entrepreneurship, thriving requires balance, rhythm, and self-awareness.

1. The Seasons of Business: Sprinting and Stillness

Like the Sahara's extremes of scorching heat and cool nights, your business operates in **seasons**. Sometimes you sprint, throwing everything you've got into the moment. Other times, you step back, breathe, and reflect. The secret to longevity? Knowing how to honor both rhythms.

Sprint Season:

These are the high-energy moments—launching a product, closing a deal, or running a major campaign. Sprints are exhilarating, but they demand focus, resilience, and short-term sacrifices.

Example:

Emma, an online coach, spent a month preparing for her first group program launch. Her days were packed with late-night emails, social media strategy, and recording content. She embraced the grind, knowing she had scheduled downtime after the launch to recover.

Reflect & Recharge Season:

After the sprint comes a quieter season to recover, evaluate, and refine. This is where growth truly happens—by stepping back and realigning with your vision.

Example:

Post-launch, Emma took a week off to rest, journal, and evaluate what worked and what didn't. She spent time with family, reconnected with her "why," and returned to work refreshed and inspired.

Actionable Insight:

Every business has its natural ebb and flow. Plan for these cycles and trust that rest isn't slacking—it's fueling your next sprint.

2. The Energy Compass: How to Prioritize Like a Pro

In the desert, wandering aimlessly wastes valuable energy—and in business, wasting time on the wrong tasks does the same. Success comes from knowing where to direct your focus.

Enter the Eisenhower Matrix:

This simple framework helps you sort your tasks by urgency and importance, ensuring your energy goes where it matters most:

- **Urgent & Important**: Do these immediately. They move the needle.
  Example: Handling a client emergency or meeting a pressing deadline.

- **Important but Not Urgent**: Schedule these thoughtfully. They're essential for long-term growth.
  Example: Developing your next product or building partnerships.

- **Urgent but Not Important**: Delegate these to free yourself for high-impact work.
  Example: Managing admin tasks or responding to routine emails.

- **Not Urgent & Not Important**: Eliminate these energy-draining distractions. *Example: Mindlessly scrolling social media or tweaking minor website details.*

	Urgent	Not Urgent
Important	**Do it** Things with clear deadlines and consequences for not taking immediate action. Examples: · Finishing a client project · Submitting a draft article · Responding to some emails · Picking up your sick kid from school	**Schedule it** Activities without a set deadline that bring you closer to your goals. Easy to procrastinate on. Examples: · Strategic planning · Professional development · Networking · Exercise
Not Important	**Delegate it** Things that need to be done, but don't require your specific skills. Busy work. Examples: · Uploading blog posts · Scheduling · Responding to some emails · Meal prep	**Delete it** Distractions that make you feel worse afterward. Can be ok but only in moderation. Examples: · Social media · Watching TV · Video games · Eating junk food

Pro Tip:

Before starting any task, ask yourself: *Does this truly move the needle?* If not, delegate or eliminate it.

3. Energy Conservation: Your Business Survival Kit

The desert is a master teacher of efficiency. Travelers survive by conserving water, staying in the shade, and traveling during the coolest hours. Likewise, smart entrepreneurs learn to manage their resources wisely to avoid burnout.

Strategies for Energy Conservation:

- **Set Boundaries**: Protect your time fiercely.
  Example: Establish non-negotiable office hours or commit to unplugging by 8 PM.

- **Delegate & Outsource**: Free yourself to focus on high-value tasks.
  Example: Hire a virtual assistant to manage emails or use automation tools for invoicing.

- **Simplify Systems**: Streamline your workflows to save time and mental energy.
  Example: Use templates for proposals, create SOPs, or batch your content creation.

Mantra: Busy doesn't mean productive. Be intentional with every ounce of energy you spend.

4. Boosting Energy: Fuel for the Long Haul

Even the most seasoned desert travelers need sustenance. In business, staying energized means fueling your **body, mind, and spirit** consistently.

Physical Energy:

Your health is your business's engine. Without it, nothing moves forward.
- *Example*: Prioritize movement (a daily walk), restful sleep, and nutrient-rich meals that keep you focused and alert.

Mental Clarity:

Recharge your mind with intentional stillness.
- *Example*: Start each day with 10 minutes of meditation or a gratitude journal to center yourself.

Purpose-Driven Motivation:

Reconnect with your "why" when energy wanes. Purpose fuels perseverance.

- *Example*: Revisit client testimonials, success stories, or the tangible impact your work creates to reignite your drive.

Pro Tip: Schedule regular "you" time. Whether it's a quiet cup of coffee, a midday workout, or an afternoon of creativity, prioritize what fuels you.

5. Oasis Achieved: The Balance of Effort and Ease

An oasis isn't just a physical refuge—it's a mindset of alignment and peace. It's the moment you realize you're giving your best without overextending yourself.

How to Create Your Oasis:

- **Flexible Rhythms Over Rigid Routines**: Build systems that adapt to your energy.
  Example: Alternate between high-focus workdays and lighter admin days to stay balanced.

- **Celebrate the Small Wins**: Recognize and reward your progress along the way.
  Example: Treat yourself to a day off or a dinner out after completing a big milestone.*

- **Say No with Confidence**: Guard your energy by turning down opportunities that don't align with your goals.

Final Thought:

In the Sahara, the oasis is a place of life and rejuvenation. In business, it's the balance between effort and rest. When you prioritize your energy and align your actions with your purpose, you'll not only navigate the journey—you'll thrive in it.

Up Next: Wellness and Mindset

As we move forward, we'll dive deeper into **Wellness and Mindset**, exploring the tools and habits that build resilience and mental clarity. Together, we'll ensure your journey is not just impactful but deeply sustainable.

Take a deep breath. You're exactly where you need to be—and the best is yet to come.

Action Items – Mastering Energy for Sustainable Success

Entrepreneurship isn't about endless hustle—it's about knowing when to sprint, when to pause, and how to sustain yourself for the long haul. Use these action steps to optimize your energy and create a business that thrives without burning you out.

1. Embrace the Seasons of Business

- Identify your **current season**—are you in a sprint (high-energy execution) or a stillness phase (reflection & recalibration)?

- Plan for recovery time **after major launches, projects, or intense work periods**.

- Schedule intentional pauses—block off time in your calendar for rest, creativity, and big-picture thinking.

2. Prioritize with the Energy Compass

- Use the **Eisenhower Matrix** to categorize your tasks by urgency and importance.

- **Eliminate or delegate** low-value tasks that drain your energy without meaningful results.

- Set a **"Move the Needle" filter**—before starting any task, ask: *Does this directly contribute to my goals?*

3. Protect & Conserve Your Energy

- **Set firm boundaries**—define work hours, unplug from tech after a certain time, and say no to distractions.

- **Outsource & automate**—delegate admin tasks, use scheduling tools, and systematize repetitive work.

- **Batch work strategically**—group similar tasks (e.g., content creation, emails, or meetings) to maximize focus.

4. Fuel Your Mind & Body for Longevity

- Prioritize **daily movement, quality sleep, and nourishing food** to sustain energy.

- Start each day with a **mindset reset**—meditation, journaling, or a gratitude practice.

- Reconnect with your **"why"** regularly—review testimonials, impact stories, or your original vision to reignite motivation.

5. Build Your Oasis: The Balance of Effort & Ease

- Design **flexible work rhythms**—alternate high-focus days with lighter admin or creative days.

- Celebrate small wins—acknowledge progress and **reward yourself** for milestones.

- **Confidently say no**—protect your time and energy by turning down commitments that don't align with your mission.

Notes & Reflection

Notes & Reflection

Chapter Fourteen

Stop #10 – Dog sled in the Antarctic...

YOU HAVE TO BE AT THE TOP OF YOUR GAME TO PARTICIPATE. ARE YOU TAKING CARE OF YOURSELF?

"Take care of your body. It's the only place you have to live." – Jim Rohn

Stop #10 – Dog Sled in the Antarctic: Are You Taking Care of Yourself?

Picture the Antarctic—vast, frigid, and unrelenting. Survival here isn't about brute force but about balance, preparation, and care. Sled dogs thrive not because they run tirelessly but because their handlers ensure they're well-fed, rested, and in peak condition. These champions are unstoppable because they're supported with care and intention.

Now, think of yourself as the leader of your own sled team—your business. You are the driving force. But here's the truth: no matter how passionate or determined you are, you can't lead your team, steer through storms, or reach your destination if you're running on empty.

In entrepreneurship, success isn't about burning yourself out for the next goal. It's about learning to care for yourself—body, mind, and soul—so you can endure the challenges, find clarity, and show up as your best self. In this chapter, we'll dive deep into the art of self-care and how it's not just necessary but critical for thriving in business and life.

1. The Foundation of Success: Self-Care is Non-Negotiable

Entrepreneurship is an endurance sport, not a sprint. Think of it like sledding through a blizzard—if you don't refuel, rest, or take care of your pack, you won't last long. But self-care isn't a one-time luxury; it's a daily discipline.

What Self-Care Really Means

It's not just about bubble baths and yoga (though those are great!). Self-care is about aligning your actions and routines with your physical, emotional, and mental needs. It's about operating from a place of *strength* rather than depletion.

- **Why It Matters:**

    - **Mental Clarity:** A well-rested mind is better at solving problems, spotting opportunities, and making decisions.

    - **Energy & Creativity:** Proper care keeps your creative engine running, fueling your business with fresh ideas and solutions.

- ○ **Resilience:** Self-care builds the stamina to bounce back after setbacks and stay grounded through uncertainty.

Example:

James, a tech entrepreneur, constantly burned the midnight oil, believing hustle was the only path to success. After months of fatigue and brain fog, he shifted his focus to prioritizing sleep, exercise, and structured downtime. The result? A noticeable boost in productivity, clarity, and his ability to lead with confidence.

2. Fueling the Engine: Physical Wellness

Your body is your business's engine. Treat it poorly, and it will sputter and stall. Like the sled dogs that rely on proper care to race across icy terrains, you must nourish, move, and rest your body to sustain your momentum.

Healthy Eating: Food as Fuel

Your body isn't a garbage disposal—it's a finely tuned machine. The right fuel leads to sharper focus, higher energy, and greater endurance.

Tips:

- Prioritize **whole, nutrient-dense foods** like lean proteins, whole grains, and colorful vegetables.

- Stay hydrated. Keep a water bottle by your side to sip throughout the day.

- Plan meals to avoid unhealthy, last-minute takeout that drags your energy down.

Example:

Sophie, a freelance designer, swapped her daily sugary snacks for whole fruits and nuts. This small shift eliminated her mid-afternoon energy crashes, helping her stay productive longer.

Exercise: Move for Strength and Clarity

Movement isn't just about physical health—it sharpens your mind, reduces stress, and increases focus.

Ideas:

- Start the day with a **10-minute stretch** or yoga session to wake up your body and mind.

- Take **short movement breaks** during the day to combat fatigue from sitting.

- Find an activity you love—dancing, swimming, cycling—to make exercise enjoyable.

Example:

After years of neglecting her health, Laura, a startup founder, committed to walking 30 minutes every morning. Not only did she notice a surge in energy, but her problem-solving skills also improved during her walks.

Sleep: The Ultimate Recharge

Sleep isn't optional—it's your superpower. Proper rest helps your brain process information, solve problems, and rejuvenate.

Tips for Better Sleep:

- Stick to a consistent sleep schedule.

- Wind down with a bedtime routine—read, journal, or meditate.

- Avoid screens an hour before bed to reduce blue light exposure.

Example:

After committing to seven hours of quality sleep, Kevin, a marketing consultant, found his mornings became his most productive time for creative work.

3. Mind and Spirit: Your Inner Strength

Entrepreneurship tests your mental and emotional fortitude. From navigating setbacks to managing stress, your ability to stay grounded is key.

Stress Management: Build Your Toolkit

Running a business comes with high highs and low lows. Managing stress ensures you don't buckle under pressure.

Stress Relief Ideas:

- **Meditate:** Start with 5 minutes of deep breathing or guided mindfulness.

- **Journal:** Write down what's overwhelming you—or focus on gratitude.

- **Disconnect:** Take regular breaks from social media and email to recharge.

Emotional Resilience: Building Strength

When challenges hit, it's easy to feel defeated. Practices like therapy, gratitude journaling, or reflecting on your purpose help you stay anchored.

Example:

Nina, a social entrepreneur, started keeping a journal of client success stories. On hard days, revisiting those stories reminded her why she started and reignited her drive.

4. The Power of Nature: Recharge with Your Environment

Sled dogs thrive in the open air, and so do we. Nature is a powerful reset button that reduces stress, boosts mood, and inspires creativity.

Ways to Reconnect with Nature:

- Take a **15-minute walk** outside every day to clear your head.

- Bring nature indoors—add plants to your workspace.

- Plan weekend escapes to hike, bike, or simply sit by the water.

Example:

Jake, a financial advisor, incorporated short outdoor walks into his day. Not only did he return with a clearer mind, but his best ideas often came during these quiet moments.

Final Thoughts: Your Well-Being is the Ultimate Investment

Much like sled dogs conquering the Antarctic, your ability to thrive depends on how well you care for yourself. Self-care isn't selfish—it's the foundation for sustainable success. When you invest in your wellness, you don't just survive—you lead, create, and build with clarity and strength.

Next up, we'll focus on building a *resilient mindset*—your mental compass for navigating challenges and steering toward success. Together, we'll prepare you to face the unpredictable with confidence and grace. Take a deep breath, step into alignment, and remember: **the leader of the sled must first care for themselves to lead the pack.**

Action Items – Prioritizing Your Well-Being for Long-Term Success

Entrepreneurship is a marathon, not a sprint. Just like sled dogs thrive with proper care, you must prioritize your well-being to sustain momentum, navigate challenges, and lead with strength. Use these action steps to ensure you're running your business from a place of energy, clarity, and resilience.

1. Make Self-Care a Non-Negotiable Practice

- **Assess your current self-care habits**—what's working, and what's missing?

- **Schedule self-care like a meeting**—block time for rest, movement, and mental recharge.

- **Reframe rest as productivity**—understand that stepping back allows you to show up stronger.

2. Fuel Your Body for Energy & Endurance

- **Upgrade your nutrition**—swap processed foods for whole, nutrient-dense meals.

- **Stay hydrated**—set reminders to drink water throughout the day.

- **Plan meals in advance** to avoid energy-draining food choices.

- **Incorporate daily movement**—even a 10-minute walk boosts energy and mental clarity.

- **Commit to consistent sleep**—establish a bedtime routine to improve sleep quality.

3. Strengthen Your Mind & Manage Stress

- **Identify your biggest stress triggers** and create strategies to manage them.

- **Start a mindfulness practice**—try deep breathing, meditation, or journaling for 5 minutes daily.

- **Take digital detox breaks**—step away from screens and notifications to reset your mind.

- **Celebrate progress**—keep a success journal to remind yourself of wins on tough days.

4. Connect with Nature for Restoration

- **Get outside daily**—a short walk in fresh air can shift your mood and perspective.

- **Bring nature into your workspace**—add plants, open windows, or listen to natural sounds.

- **Plan regular nature breaks**—weekend hikes, beach walks, or quiet time in a park.

Notes & Reflection

Notes & Reflection

CHAPTER FIFTEEN

Stop #11 – Travel the rails through the Gobi Desert...

MINDSET IS MORE THAN JUST A WORD - YOUR HABITS, ROUTINES, GOALS, AND CONSISTENCY.

"Success is the sum of small efforts, repeated day in and day out." — Robert Collier

Stop #11 – Travel the Rails Through the Gobi Desert: Mindset, Habits, Routines, Goals, and Consistency

Picture the vast, ever-changing expanse of the Gobi Desert—a landscape of extremes where survival demands adaptability, focus, and collaboration among 33 unique ecosystems. Each ecosystem thrives because it plays a role in the bigger picture, working in harmony to create balance and resilience. Your mindset is no different. It's the interconnected system of your habits, routines, goals, and consistency that determines whether you merely survive or thrive in the unpredictable terrain of life and entrepreneurship.

In this chapter, we'll explore how to cultivate a mindset as enduring and adaptable as the Gobi itself. When you master these elements, you'll not only navigate life's challenges with clarity but also create a business and life that are sustainable, impactful, and deeply fulfilling.

1. Habits: The Building Blocks of Success

Just as desert animals have evolved instinctive behaviors for survival, your habits are the small, repeated actions that enable you to succeed with ease. They conserve your mental energy and create momentum, freeing you to focus on your bigger vision.

Why Habits Matter:

- **Automation**: Habits turn important actions into effortless routines, reducing decision fatigue.

- **Compounding Results**: Over time, small daily actions add up to transformative outcomes.

- **Momentum**: Positive habits create a ripple effect, influencing your mindset and productivity.

Example:

A solopreneur struggling with disorganization created a habit of spending 10 minutes every evening organizing the next day's priorities. Within weeks, they reported feeling more in control and less stressed, freeing up energy to focus on growing their business.

How to Build Game-Changing Habits:

- **Start Small**: Begin with something so simple it feels impossible to fail, like jotting down one thing you're grateful for each day.

- **Habit Stacking**: Link new habits to existing ones. For example, after pouring your morning coffee, spend 5 minutes reviewing your goals.

- **Track and Reward**: Use a habit tracker to celebrate your progress and stay motivated.

2. Routines: The Framework of Your Ecosystem

In the Gobi, interconnected ecosystems create structure and balance. Routines do the same for your life, reducing chaos and promoting flow. They allow you to intentionally allocate energy to the things that matter most.

Why Routines Matter:

- **Efficiency**: A well-structured day eliminates wasted time and reduces decision fatigue.

- **Alignment**: Routines keep you focused on your priorities, ensuring you work *on* your business, not just *in* it.

- **Resilience**: Predictable structures create stability during uncertain times.

Example:

An overwhelmed nonprofit founder implemented a morning routine that included 20 minutes of journaling and goal review. This practice helped them start the day with clarity, focus, and a renewed sense of purpose.

How to Design Purposeful Routines:

- **Morning Rituals**: Start your day with intention—try meditation, exercise, or gratitude journaling.

- **Batch Similar Tasks**: Group activities like emails or content creation to maximize focus.

- **Evening Reflections**: End the day by reviewing wins, lessons, and plans for tomorrow.

- **Flexibility**: Adjust routines to fit your current season, just like the desert adapts to shifting climates.

3. Goals: Your Compass in the Desert

The Gobi Desert is vast and treacherous—without a clear direction, it's easy to get lost. Goals are your compass, guiding you toward your aspirations with clarity and purpose.

Why Goals Matter:

- **Focus**: Goals align your actions with your vision, ensuring your energy is spent intentionally.

- **Motivation**: A clear destination inspires action, even when the path feels difficult.

- **Progress**: Goals create measurable milestones to celebrate along the journey.

Example:

A graphic designer set a SMART goal to secure five new clients within three months. By breaking the goal into smaller actions—networking, outreach, and portfolio updates—they not only hit the target but gained confidence in their process.

How to Set Goals that Stick:

- **Start with Your Vision**: Envision where you want to be in 5 or 10 years and reverse-engineer the steps to get there.

- **Make Them SMART**: Specific, Measurable, Achievable, Relevant, and Time-bound goals increase clarity and accountability.

- **Break It Down**: Turn long-term goals into weekly or daily tasks to stay focused and avoid overwhelm.

4. Consistency: Thriving Through Rhythm and Repetition

The Gobi thrives on predictable rhythms—seasonal shifts, animal migrations, and plant cycles all work together to sustain life in extremes. Likewise, consistency is the rhythm that sustains your success over time.

Why Consistency Matters:

- **Momentum**: Small, steady actions compound into significant achievements.

- **Trust**: Showing up regularly builds credibility with your audience, clients, and team.

- **Mastery**: Repetition hones your skills and increases confidence.

Example:

A blogger committed to posting once a week for a year, even when it felt like no one was reading. By staying consistent, they built an engaged audience, and opportunities for collaborations and paid writing gigs began to roll in.

How to Stay Consistent:

- **Focus on the Process**: Don't get lost in results—focus on showing up and improving each day.

- **Use Accountability**: Share your goals with a trusted peer, mentor, or coach.

- **Prepare for Setbacks**: Missing a day or two doesn't mean failure. Adjust, recommit, and keep moving.

- **Celebrate the Journey**: Every small win is proof of your progress—acknowledge and appreciate them.

5. Accountability: Your Trusted Guide in the Desert

Even the most experienced explorers rely on guides to navigate the unpredictable terrain of the Gobi. Accountability acts as your guide, keeping you aligned with your goals and helping you course-correct when needed.

Why Accountability Matters:

- **Clarity**: Others can offer perspective and identify blind spots.

- **Motivation**: Knowing someone is counting on you boosts follow-through.

- **Support**: Accountability partners provide encouragement during tough times.

Example:

A tech founder joined a peer accountability group, sharing weekly goals and progress. The structure helped them stay on track and tackle projects they'd been procrastinating on for months.

Ways to Build Accountability:

- **Partner Up**: Exchange progress updates with a peer or friend.

- **Join a Group**: Mastermind groups or community circles offer collective encouragement.

- **Track Your Progress**: Use tools like journals or apps to monitor your journey.

- **Work with a Coach**: A coach provides expert guidance tailored to your unique needs.

Final Thoughts: Thrive Like the Gobi

Just as the Gobi Desert has evolved into a resilient, thriving ecosystem, you have the power to cultivate a mindset that sustains and inspires you. With habits, routines, goals, consistency, and accountability working together, you create a foundation strong enough to endure challenges and flexible enough to adapt to change.

Remember: progress isn't about grand gestures—it's about small, intentional steps repeated over time. Embrace the journey, celebrate the growth, and trust in your ability to build a legacy as enduring as the desert itself.

Next Stop: The Final Break After the 3rd Challenge. Take this time to reflect, recharge, and prepare for the road ahead. The adventure is just beginning, and you are more ready than ever to conquer what lies ahead.

Action Items – Cultivating a Resilient Mindset for Success

Like the Gobi Desert, your success depends on an ecosystem of habits, routines, goals, consistency, and accountability. Use these action steps to build a mindset that not only survives challenges but thrives in any environment.

1. Strengthen Your Habits for Long-Term Success

- **Identify one habit** that will improve your energy, focus, or productivity.

- **Start small**—choose an action so easy you can't fail (e.g., writing one goal down each morning).

- **Use habit stacking**—attach new habits to existing routines (e.g., review your goals after your morning coffee).

- **Track progress** with a journal or app to stay motivated.

2. Design Routines That Work for You

- **Audit your daily routines**—where can you create more structure or efficiency?

- **Create a simple morning ritual** to set the tone for your day (e.g., journaling, stretching, or deep breathing).

- **Batch similar tasks** to improve focus and productivity (e.g., dedicate specific time blocks for emails, meetings, or creative work).

- **End your day intentionally**—reflect on wins and set priorities for tomorrow.

3. Set Goals That Keep You Focused & Motivated

- **Define your big vision**—what does success look like in 1, 5, or 10 years?

- **Break it down**—turn long-term goals into monthly, weekly, and daily actions.

- **Use the SMART method**—make goals Specific, Measurable, Achievable, Relevant, and Time-bound.

- **Celebrate milestones**—acknowledge small wins to stay motivated.

4. Build Consistency to Create Momentum

- **Commit to a process**—focus on showing up daily rather than chasing immediate results.

- **Eliminate excuses**—identify common obstacles and plan for how to overcome them.

- **Use accountability**—share your commitments with someone who will keep you on track.

- **Give yourself grace**—miss a day? Reset and keep going. Progress is built over time.

5. Create Accountability for Ongoing Success

- **Find an accountability partner**—check in regularly to share goals and progress.

- **Join a community or mastermind group** for motivation and collective wisdom.

- **Use a tracking system**—journals, apps, or spreadsheets help you stay accountable.

- **Consider working with a coach** to gain expert guidance and support.

Notes & Reflection

Notes & Reflection

CHAPTER SIXTEEN

Break after completing the 3rd Challenge – Energy, Wellness and Mindset

"Greatness is built on consistent, small actions, repeated relentlessly over time." – Robert Collier

Break After Completing the 3rd Challenge: Energy, Wellness, and Mindset

Congratulations! You've just reached a pivotal moment in your entrepreneurial journey. As you step off this train, having traversed uncharted territories, you're not just standing still. Your heart is fuller, your vision clearer, and your spirit lighter from all the growth you've embraced. You're no longer just a dreamer—you're a builder, a creator, and an impact maker.

This chapter is all about integration—bringing everything together. It's time to anchor the lessons you've learned about energy, wellness, and mindset so that you can step forward with clarity, strength, and resilience. The groundwork you've laid isn't just preparation for what's to come—it's the fuel for the next phase of your journey.

1. Energy: Sustain for the Long Haul

Building your dream is a marathon, not a sprint. Success in entrepreneurship isn't about constant hustle—it's about sustaining energy over the long term. Just like the explorers who journeyed across the Sahara Desert, we learned that energy is a finite resource. It needs to be conserved, channeled, and replenished intentionally. Launching a purpose-driven business requires bursts of creativity, strategic thinking, and persistence—but it also requires downtime for restoration.

Lesson: Balance Action with Restoration

Your mission will demand intense bursts of focus, but success comes when you balance pushing forward with giving yourself time to recharge. Rest isn't a luxury—it's essential for maintaining momentum and preventing burnout.

Example:

Consider an entrepreneur launching a social impact app. She dedicated her mornings to focused creative work, where she could pour all her energy into brainstorming and problem-solving. In the afternoons, she engaged in collaborative meetings to refine ideas. Evenings were reserved for self-care, such as yoga, reading, and spending time with loved ones. This deliberate balance of work and rest allowed her to keep her energy high and her creativity flowing without burning out.

Key Takeaway:

Energy is sacred. Plan your work in alignment with your natural rhythms, ensuring you're intentional about both action and rest.

2. Habits & Routines: Build Unshakable Structures

Think back to the Gobi Desert, where thriving ecosystems depend on consistent, interconnected systems. Your habits and routines work the same way. They act as the foundational structures that support your success as you navigate the chaos of entrepreneurship. When things get turbulent, having strong habits keeps you grounded and moving forward.

Lesson: Create Anchors for Stability

In the unpredictable world of entrepreneurship, strong habits and routines become your anchors. They reduce overwhelm, streamline your day, and ensure that you're making consistent progress toward your vision.

Example:

A podcaster launching a new show used a "theme day" routine to stay organized. Mondays were reserved for research, Wednesdays for recording, and Fridays for editing and promoting episodes. By adhering to this routine, the podcaster created consistency, reduced overwhelm, and ensured that each episode was released on time with high-quality content that resonated with her growing audience.

Key Takeaway:

Habits and routines act as anchors, keeping you stable in the storm of entrepreneurship. They ensure progress even when life gets messy.

3. Wellness: Your Non-Negotiable Foundation

Your wellness is your greatest asset. Much like the Antarctic sled dogs, whose endurance was a direct result of being properly cared for and fueled, your physical, mental, and emotional well-being is critical to your success. Neglecting your wellness means risking your ability to sustain your energy, creativity, and resilience.

Lesson: Prioritize Your Peak Performance

Launching your business will push you to your limits. But if you neglect your well-being, you'll quickly find yourself depleted. You need mental clarity, emotional balance, and physical stamina to execute your vision sustainably.

Example:

A founder launching a community-driven art project made wellness a non-negotiable part of her routine. She committed to getting 7–8 hours of sleep each night, eating nourishing meals, and practicing daily meditation. This intentional focus on her well-being helped her stay energized, stay connected with collaborators, and navigate both the highs and lows of the launch with clarity and resilience.

Key Takeaway:

Wellness isn't just a personal priority—it's a business strategy. When you take care of yourself, you show up sharper, stronger, and more resilient.

Reflection: Look How Far You've Come

Before we dive into the next phase, take a moment to pause and reflect on the progress you've made:

- **Energy:** How have you learned to manage your focus and sustain your momentum throughout the ups and downs of this journey?

- **Habits:** Have you built routines that anchor your progress and keep you on track even in chaotic moments?

- **Wellness:** Are you prioritizing your mind, body, and spirit to stay at your peak performance?

These three pillars—energy, routines, and wellness—are interconnected. Together, they form the bedrock for a sustainable, purpose-driven business. As you take the next step toward launching, these lessons will not only ensure your survival in the entrepreneurial world, but will also empower you to thrive and create the lasting impact you've envisioned.

Preparing for What's Next: The Launch

With this solid foundation, you're ready to take the leap from preparation to execution. Launching your venture is all about translating your vision into reality. Everything you've learned so far is the groundwork for this moment.

In the next chapter, we'll tackle:

- **Crafting a clear, actionable launch plan** that aligns with your values and your vision.

- **Building systems** for smooth operations and scalable growth.

- Practical tools to help you **navigate challenges** and stay consistent throughout this crucial phase.

Final Thoughts: You're Ready

Take a deep breath and look back at how far you've come. You've done the work—built the mindset, habits, and resilience to thrive. Now, it's time to take bold, inspired action and launch the legacy you've been dreaming of.

You're no longer the person who started this journey. You're stronger, wiser, and more capable than you've ever been. It's time to create something extraordinary.

Next Stop: Launch Your Legacy

Action Items for This Chapter:

1. Plan Your Energy Management:

- Identify your peak energy times during the day (morning, afternoon, evening).

- Design your work schedule to align with these natural rhythms, ensuring you're doing creative or high-focus tasks during your peak times and saving routine or less demanding tasks for when your energy is lower.

- **Action:** Plan one full week of work, factoring in breaks and downtime to avoid burnout.

2. Create Unshakable Routines:

- Build a weekly routine that supports your goals. Use a "theme day" structure or designate certain times for specific tasks.

- **Action:** Develop a weekly schedule that includes daily rituals like morning reflections, time-blocking for deep work, and evening relaxation.

3. Prioritize Wellness:

- Incorporate daily wellness routines—sleep, nutrition, exercise, and mental health practices like meditation or journaling.

- **Action:** Schedule wellness activities into your daily routine and commit to one month of consistent wellness practices.

4. Reflect and Adjust:

- Take a moment at the end of each week to assess how your energy, routines, and wellness are affecting your progress.

- **Action:** Set aside 30 minutes at the end of the week for a personal review.

Reflect on how you managed your energy, which routines worked, and what wellness habits need adjusting.

Notes & Reflection

Notes & Reflection

CHAPTER SEVENTEEN

Returning home...

YOU'VE CHANGED. YOU'VE GROWN. IT'S TIME TO BRING IT ALL TOGETHER AND LAUNCH YOUR BUSINESS.

"You can't go back and change the beginning, but you can start where you are and change the ending." – C.S. Lewis

Returning Home – You've Changed, You've Grown, and Now It's Time to Launch

After navigating deserts, jungles, and mountains, you've returned to where it all began—but this time, you're different. You're not the same person who set out with curiosity and questions. You've grown stronger, gained clarity, and uncovered a vision that is now ready to come to life.

This chapter is about embracing who you've become, pulling together everything you've learned, and stepping boldly into your purpose-driven business. It's time to align your growth, solidify your plans, and launch your legacy with confidence and intention.

1. You're Not Who You Were—And That's Your Superpower

Transformation changes everything: how you see yourself, how you approach your mission, and even the relationships around you. Growth isn't always easy, but it's always worth it. The person you've become is the person your vision needs.

Share Your Journey

Let those around you know how your growth benefits not just you but the world you want to impact. By opening up about your transformation, you can bring others along for the ride.

Example:
A community organizer returning from a leadership retreat found that her new focus on saying "no" to distractions confused her colleagues. She explained how protecting her time allowed her to focus on bigger goals for their cause, turning initial resistance into collective support.

Realign Your Circle

Not everyone is meant to walk this next chapter with you—and that's okay. Seek out those who challenge, inspire, and celebrate your growth.

Example:

An artist who wanted to grow her creative business noticed that some of her friendships revolved around negativity. By joining a mastermind for creatives, she found a circle of people who motivated her, shared resources, and supported her vision for building a meaningful, sustainable art brand.

Key Takeaway: Your transformation is your strength. Embrace it, communicate it, and surround yourself with people who align with your future—not just your past.

2. Pulling It All Together: Your Business Plan

A business plan isn't just paperwork—it's your blueprint for building a venture rooted in purpose and sustainability. It's where your experiences, values, and vision combine into a clear, actionable strategy.

Clarify Your Mission and Vision

Your mission is the "why" of your business, and your vision is the change you aim to create. Let them guide everything you do.

Example:

A social entrepreneur launching an ethical skincare brand framed her mission as: "Empowering consumers to choose beauty without harm." Her vision? A world where ethical, sustainable products are the norm, not the exception.

Know Your People

Your audience isn't just a demographic—it's a community of people whose dreams, challenges, and values align with what you offer. Speak directly to their hearts.

Example:

A photographer focused on capturing authentic moments for LGBTQ+ couples highlighted her inclusive approach in her messaging. By emphasizing her understanding of her audience's unique stories, she built trust and became their go-to choice.

Make Your Numbers Work

Your financial plan doesn't have to be complicated, but it does need to be clear. Budget for your launch, project your revenue, and know your path to profitability.

Example:

A food truck owner used data from local festivals to estimate demand and set prices. By planning smartly, she covered her costs and made a profit at her very first event.

Key Takeaway: Your business plan isn't just a task; it's the foundation that turns your purpose into a sustainable reality.

3. The Launch: Ready, Set, Go

Your launch isn't the final step; it's the beginning of something extraordinary. Start with intention, focus on progress over perfection, and trust that you'll refine and grow as you go.

Simplify and Start Strong

You don't need every detail perfect on Day 1. Focus on your core offering and the essentials, then build from there.

Example:

A career coach launched her business with a single workshop, gathering feedback to refine her services before rolling out a full coaching program.

Create Momentum

Treat your launch as the spark for a movement. Build excitement, engage early adopters, and let your audience help amplify your mission.

Example:

A founder launching a line of eco-friendly planners hosted a "launch week" on social media with live demonstrations, giveaways, and customer stories. Her audience felt like co-creators in her journey, spreading the word far beyond her expectations.

Key Takeaway: Your launch is your opportunity to invite others into your story. Make it meaningful, and let your passion be contagious.

4. Balancing Your New Life

Building your business is exciting, but it's also demanding. To sustain your creativity and drive, you'll need to prioritize balance. Remember, you're creating something lasting—not just sprinting to the finish line.

Create a Grounding Routine

Start your day with intention. Whether it's through mindfulness, movement, or planning, a consistent morning practice keeps you aligned with your purpose.

Example:
A writer launching her first book spent 10 minutes each morning journaling about her vision and goals. This routine kept her focused and inspired, even when challenges arose.

Block Your Time

Time-blocking prevents overwhelm and ensures you're giving attention to what matters most.

Example:
A tech founder reserved her mornings for deep work on product development and her afternoons for team collaboration. This approach maximized her productivity and minimized distractions.

Rest as a Ritual

Your business thrives when you do. Build intentional rest into your schedule, and don't treat it as optional.

Example:
A marketing consultant took every Sunday off for family time and outdoor adventures. This weekly reset left her recharged and ready to tackle the week ahead.

Key Takeaway: Balance is the secret to longevity. When you care for yourself, you can sustain your energy, creativity, and impact.

5. You're Ready—The World Is Waiting

This journey has brought you to this moment. You've grown, learned, and built the foundation you need to launch with confidence. Now, it's time to step boldly into your purpose.

Launching your business isn't just about creating something new—it's about stepping fully into who you're meant to be. This is your legacy, your chance to leave the world better than you found it.

Take the leap. The world is ready for what only you can bring.

Let's make it happen.

Notes & Reflection

Notes & Reflection

CHAPTER EIGHTEEN

Common Business Terms Defined

A

- **Accounts Payable** - Money your business owes to others, like suppliers or contractors. It's what you still need to pay out.

- **Accounts Receivable** - Money owed to your business by customers who haven't paid yet. It's like an IOU that you expect to collect soon.

- **Affiliate Marketing** - When you partner with other people or businesses who promote your product, and you pay them a commission for each sale they bring in.

- **Angel Investors** - Individuals who provide funding to early-stage businesses in exchange for ownership equity. They help businesses get off the ground when they need it most.

- **API (Application Programming Interface)** - A way for different software applications to talk to each other. It's like a bridge that connects your app with other tools or services, making them work together seamlessly.

- **Assets** - Things your business owns that have value, like cash, equipment, property, or intellectual property such as trademarks.

- **Artificial Intelligence (AI)** - Technology that allows computers to perform tasks that normally require human intelligence, like recognizing speech or solving problems.

B

- **Balance Sheet** - A snapshot of your business's finances at a specific moment. It shows what you own (assets), what you owe (liabilities), and what's left over (equity).

- **B2B (Business to Business)** - A business model where your company sells products or services to other businesses rather than individual consumers.

- **B2C (Business to Consumer)** - A business model where your company sells products or services directly to individual customers.

- **Big Data** - Extremely large sets of data that businesses collect and analyze to make better decisions. It's all about finding patterns in massive amounts of information.

- **Blockchain** - A secure way of recording information that's impossible to change. It's often used for digital currencies but can also be applied to industries like supply chains.

- **Blue Ocean Strategy** - A strategy focused on finding new, uncontested market spaces where competition is minimal. It's all about creating something unique.

- **Bootstrapping** - Starting and growing a business with little to no outside funding. It's all about being resourceful and making the most of what you have.

- **Brand Awareness** - How familiar people are with your business and what it offers. It's about making sure your name pops up when they need what you provide.

- **Branding** - The feeling people get when they think of your business. It's your logo, colors, and even the way you talk to customers, shaping how they see you.

- **Brand Loyalty** - When customers stick with your business and keep coming back because they trust and love what you offer.

- **Break-even Point** - The moment your revenue equals your costs. Your business isn't losing money but isn't making a profit yet either.

- **Budget** - A plan for how you'll spend your money. It helps you prioritize, avoid overspending, and make sure you've got what you need for the long run.

- **Business Ecosystem** - The network of organizations—suppliers, customers, and partners—that interact and create value together. Think of it as a supportive community.

- **Business Ethics** - The moral principles that guide how you run your company. It's about doing what's right, not just what's profitable.

- **Business Model** - The strategy your business uses to make money by offering value to customers. It's the way your business operates and turns a profit.

- **Business Plan** - A written document outlining your business goals, strategies, target market, and financial projections. It's your roadmap to success.

C

- **Call to Action (CTA)** - A prompt that encourages your audience to take the next step. Whether it's "Sign Up" or "Buy Now," it guides them to take action.

- **Cash Flow** - The movement of money in and out of your business. Positive cash flow means more is coming in than going out—always a good sign!

- **Competitive Advantage** - What sets your business apart from the competition. It's the special thing that makes people choose you over others.

- **Competitive Analysis** - The process of researching your competitors to understand their strengths and weaknesses so you can find ways to stand out.

- **Content Marketing** - Creating valuable, useful content to attract and engage your target audience. Whether it's blog posts, videos, or social media, it's all about telling your story.

- **Corporation** - A business that's a separate legal entity from its owners. It can own property, take on debt, and be held responsible for its actions separately from the people running it.

- **Crowdfunding** - Raising money for your business by getting small contributions from a large number of people, usually through online platforms.

- **Cryptocurrency** - Digital money that uses blockchain technology to operate securely. It's decentralized, meaning no bank or government controls it.

- **Customer Journey** - The entire experience someone has with your business, from hearing about you for the first time to making a purchase and beyond.

- **Customer Retention** - Keeping the customers you've already gained by building relationships so they continue to choose your business over time.

- **Customer Service** - How you treat your customers before, during, and after they buy from you. A happy customer is a loyal customer!

D

- **Delegation** - Letting go of some tasks and trusting others to do them. It frees you up to focus on the big picture while building a strong team.

- **Direct Sales** - Selling products directly to consumers, usually face-to-face or through personal contact, without using a retail store or middleman.

- **Disruption** - When a new product or service changes the way an industry operates. It's about shaking things up and challenging the status quo.

- **Diversification** - Expanding into new markets or offering new products to reduce risk and increase growth opportunities.

E

- **E-commerce** - Selling products or services online. It's having a virtual storefront that customers can visit anytime, anywhere.

- **Email Marketing** - Staying in touch with customers by sending newsletters, promotions, or updates straight to their inbox.

- **Equity** - The value left in your business after you subtract liabilities from assets. It's the ownership stake you or your shareholders hold.

- **Exit Strategy** - Your plan for how you'll leave or sell your business when the time is right, offering options for the future.

- **Expenses** - The costs of running your business, like rent, supplies, or software. Keeping track of them helps you stay on top of your finances.

F

- **Freelancer** - Someone who works independently, offering their skills or services to multiple clients without being tied to a single employer.

G

- **Goal Setting** - Establishing milestones to give your business direction, whether it's growing sales, launching new products, or building a stronger team.

- **Gross Profit** - The money left after subtracting the cost of making your product from your revenue. It's what you have before paying expenses like rent or salaries.

I

- **Innovation** - Coming up with new ideas or ways of doing things that improve your business. It could be a new product, process, or simply a fresh approach.

- **Inventory** - The products or materials you have on hand to sell to customers. It's what's ready to go when someone places an order.

J

- **Joint Venture** - When two or more businesses team up on a specific project, sharing resources, expertise, and profits.

K

- **KPIs (Key Performance Indicators)** - Measurable values that show how effectively your business is achieving key objectives. Think of them as a scorecard to track progress.

L

- **Lean Business** - A business model focused on cutting waste, being efficient, and only using resources that add value to customers.

- **Leadership** - Guiding your team and helping everyone work toward a common goal. Leadership is about inspiring people to do their best.

- **Liabilities** - The debts or obligations your business owes, like loans, unpaid bills, or salaries you need to pay.

M

- **Machine Learning** - A type of AI where computers learn from data and get better at tasks without being explicitly programmed. It's like teaching a computer to learn by example!

- **Marketing** - Telling the world about your business by sharing your story and attracting people who will love what you do.

- **Marketing Funnel** - The path customers take from first hearing about your business to making a purchase. It starts wide and narrows as people move closer to buying.

- **Mission Statement** - The heart of your business. It's why you do what you do and the difference you want to make in the world.

- **MVP (Minimum Viable Product)** - The simplest version of your product that you can launch to test the waters, with just enough features to gather feedback.

N

- **Net Profit** - The money left after all expenses are paid. It's the actual profit you keep after covering everything from materials to taxes.

- **Net Worth** - The big-picture number for your business: your total assets minus total liabilities, showing your business's overall value.

- **Networking** - Building relationships with people who can help you grow your business. It's about having conversations, sharing ideas, and finding ways to support each other.

- **Niche Market** - A small, specific group of people with unique needs that your business serves. Instead of appealing to everyone, you focus on a particular group.

O

- **Outsourcing** - Hiring someone outside your company to handle certain tasks. It's getting expert help so you can focus on what you do best.

P

- **P&L (Profit and Loss) Statement** - A simple way to see how much money your business made and spent over a period of time. It shows whether your business made a profit or took a loss.

- **Partnership** - When two or more people own a business together, sharing responsibility, profits, and decision-making.

- **Pay-per-click (PPC)** - An online advertising model where you only pay when someone clicks on your ad. It's a cost-effective way to reach your target audience.

- **Pitch Deck** - A presentation used by startups to showcase their business idea to potential investors. It's your business's elevator pitch but with slides.

- **Pricing Strategy** - How you decide what to charge for your products or services. It's about balancing value with profitability.

- **Product Lifecycle** - The journey your product goes through, from launch to growth, maturity, and eventual decline.

- **Profit** - The money left over after you've paid your bills. It's your reward for running a successful business!

- **Profit Margin** - The percentage of revenue that turns into profit after all expenses are covered. It shows how efficiently your business is making money.

R

- **Retargeting** - An advertising strategy that shows ads to people who have already visited your website, reminding them to come back and take another look.

- **Revenue** - The money your business makes from selling its products or services. Think of it as the cash that keeps the business wheels turning!

- **ROI (Return on Investment)** - A way to measure how much value you're getting from the money you spend. It's about making sure your investments in time, money, or effort are worth it!

S

- **SaaS (Software as a Service)** - Software that's available online instead of being downloaded. Customers pay a subscription to use it without having to install anything.

- **Sales** - The process of helping people buy your product or service. It's about solving problems and making lives better with what you offer.

- **Scalability** - How easily your business can grow without running into too many problems. A scalable business can handle growth smoothly.

- **SEO (Search Engine Optimization)** - The practice of improving your website so it ranks higher in search engine results. It's making sure your business shows up when people search for what you offer.

- **Social Media Strategy** - Your plan for using platforms like Instagram, Facebook, or LinkedIn to build your brand, connect with customers, and grow your business.

- **Sole Proprietorship** - The simplest form of business ownership—just you, running your business. You get all the profits, but you're also responsible for any losses.

- **Stakeholders** - The people or groups who have an interest in your business, like customers, employees, investors, or the community around you.

- **Supply Chain** - The process of getting your products from raw materials to the final product that customers can buy. It includes everything from suppliers to shipping.

- **Sustainability** - Creating products or services in a way that doesn't harm the environment or use up resources, ensuring your business can thrive long-term.

- **SWOT (Strengths, Weaknesses, Opportunities, Threats) Analysis** - A tool for identifying your business's strengths, weaknesses, opportunities, and threats. It's a simple way to assess where you stand.

T

- **Target Market** - The group of people most likely to buy your product or service. They're your ideal customers, and you focus your marketing on them.

- **Thought Leadership** - Being seen as an expert in your industry, someone people look to for insights, advice, and innovative ideas.

V

- **Value Proposition** - The promise you make to customers about what you'll deliver and why they should choose you over anyone else.

- **Venture Capital** - Money invested in startups and small businesses with high growth potential, usually by specialized firms looking for big returns.

- **Vision Statement** - Your big dream for the future. It's where you want your business to go and what success looks like to you.

W

- **Working Capital** - The money your business has to cover day-to-day expenses. It's the funds available to keep things running smoothly.

CHAPTER NINETEEN

Philosophy and Creed

Our Philosophy

At the heart of everything we do is a simple belief: big ideas, when paired with intentional action, can create meaningful and lasting change. We believe in empowering unconventional thinkers and passionate doers to transform their dreams into ventures that matter—not just to themselves, but to their communities and the world.

We approach every challenge with integrity, compassion, and a focus on sustainability. Success isn't just about reaching the top; it's about building something that aligns with your values, positively impacts others, and stands the test of time.

Our philosophy is rooted in three core principles:

Purpose First: True fulfillment comes from aligning your work with your values and the change you want to see in the world.

Sustainability Matters: Great ideas are built to last, fostering long-term growth and impact.

Progress Over Perfection: Every step forward is a victory. Resilience, adaptability, and intention create the foundation for success.

We believe that everyone has the potential to leave a legacy. Our role is to guide, support, and empower you to make yours a reality.

Creed

We are the Dreamers and Doers.

We believe in the power of big ideas and bold action.

We are the Rebels and Misfits.

We challenge the status quo, daring to create what others say cannot be done.

We are the Changemakers and Creators.

We build with purpose, crafting sustainable legacies that make the world a better place.

We believe in purpose over profit.

Our work serves a higher calling—one that positively impacts lives and communities.

We honor progress over perfection.

We know that every step, no matter how small, brings us closer to creating something extraordinary.

We embrace resilience and adaptability.

Challenges fuel our growth; setbacks spark our innovation.

We act with integrity, kindness, and empathy.

Our success is measured by the positive impact we leave behind.

We are united by a vision: to empower, to inspire, and to lead.

Together, we create businesses, movements, and lives that truly matter.

This is our creed. This is who we are.

CHAPTER TWENTY

About the Author

K risti Smith is a celebrated author and internationally renowned business coach who has dedicated her career to empowering unconventional thinkers and passionate doers. Known for her unique approach, Kristi marries powerful business, life, and leadership strategies to help individuals transform their big ideas into sustainable ventures that create lasting, positive impact on their communities and the world.

Her work has supported thousands of changemakers worldwide—visionaries, creatives, and leaders—equipping them with practical, foundational principles to expand their businesses and live with purpose.

But Kristi's journey hasn't always been smooth sailing. She's built businesses, pivoted when the vision changed, and even faced the reality of closing ventures that no longer served their purpose. She's climbed the corporate ladder, encountered health challenges, and navigated life's inevitable ups and downs. Through it all, Kristi discovered a universal truth: the key to sustainable success lies in returning to the basics—clarity, strategy, and unwavering purpose.

Kristi's mission is simple yet profound: to inspire and equip changemakers to transform their passion into action and their ideas into impact. Whether guiding individuals through business coaching, mentoring, or leadership development, her goal is to help others create ventures that are not just profitable but meaningful and sustainable for the long term.

With Kristi's guidance, big dreams become bold realities—and together, those realities change the world.

Empowering Unconventional Thinkers to Build a Better World
In Kristi's own words:
I've always been drawn to the art of creating something meaningful. From my early days selling catalpa worms to fishermen, babysitting neighborhood kids, and honing my Girl Scout cookie sales pitch, I learned that creativity, hard work, and connection could turn even the simplest ideas into something impactful.

That entrepreneurial spark grew with me. As a teenager and young adult, I immersed myself in industries like retail, food service, and customer service, learning the importance of adaptability, teamwork, and delivering value. These experiences laid the foundation for everything I do today—helping people like you take your big ideas and turn them into ventures that matter.

Even as I climbed the corporate ladder in accounting—moving from intern to Payroll Supervisor, Revenue Manager, and beyond—I knew I wanted more than just a career. I wanted to create, inspire, and empower. That drive led me to leave Corporate America in 1999 to start my own Accounting and Bookkeeping Firm, serving clients across four states and growing alongside them. Through my work, I realized that my passion wasn't just in the numbers—it was in helping people bring their dreams to life.

Over the years, I've built, pivoted, and closed businesses. I've faced life's ups and downs, balancing professional success with personal challenges, including chronic health conditions. These experiences taught me that success isn't about having all the answers upfront—it's about resilience, adaptability, and always coming back to your core purpose.

Today, my mission is simple but profound: to empower unconventional thinkers and passionate doers to transform their big ideas into sustainable ventures that positively impact their communities and the world.

As your business coach, I bring decades of hands-on experience, a deep understanding of what it takes to succeed, and a genuine belief in the power of your vision. Together, we'll focus on practical, foundational strategies that align with your goals and values.

Whether you're just starting out, looking to pivot, or aiming to scale, I'm here to help you:

- Clarify your vision.

- Build a sustainable plan.

- Create something that not only thrives but makes a difference.

This work isn't just about profit—it's about purpose. It's about building businesses that inspire change and leave legacies.

Beyond coaching, I've written over 100 books and developed more than 150 courses, blending creativity with practical guidance. My passion for community runs deep—I've volunteered with numerous organizations and initiatives to create positive impact wherever I can. These values—kindness, compassion, empathy, and honesty—guide everything I do.

When I'm not working with changemakers like you, I'm likely on the golf course, cheering for Notre Dame, or curled up with a book and a chai latte.

Your dreams matter. Your ideas matter. And I believe you have what it takes to create something extraordinary. Let's work together to make your vision a reality—and build a legacy that truly makes a difference.

To stay in touch, Kristi highly recommends that you subscribe to her monthly newsletter, *The Kristi Smith Letter,* which is written by hand, printed, and mailed to you. You can get a thirty-day free trial by visiting www.kristismithcoaching.com/free-trial